BBC Radiophonic Workshop
A Retrospective

Praise for the series:

It was only a matter of time before a clever publisher realized that there is an audience for whom *Exile on Main Street* or *Electric Ladyland* are as significant and worthy of study as *The Catcher in the Rye* or *Middlemarch* ... The series ... is freewheeling and eclectic, ranging from minute rock-geek analysis to idiosyncratic personal celebration
—*The New York Times Book Review*

Ideal for the rock geek who thinks liner notes just aren't enough
—*Rolling Stone*

One of the coolest publishing imprints on the planet
—*Bookslut*

These are for the insane collectors out there who appreciate fantastic design, well-executed thinking, and things that make your house look cool. Each volume in this series takes a seminal album and breaks it down in startling minutiae.
We love these. We are huge nerds
—*Vice*

A brilliant series ... each one a work of real love
—*NME* (UK)

Passionate, obsessive, and smart
—*Nylon*

Religious tracts for the rock 'n' roll faithful
—*Boldtype*

[A] consistently excellent series
—*Uncut* (UK)

We … aren't naive enough to think that we're your only source for reading about music (but if we had our way … watch out). For those of you who really like to know everything there is to know about an album, you'd do well to check out Bloomsbury's "33 1/3" series of books
—*Pitchfork*

For almost twenty years, the Thirty-Three-and-a-Third series of music books has focused on individual albums by acts well known (Bob Dylan, Nirvana, Abba, Radiohead), cultish (Neutral Milk Hotel, Throbbing Gristle, Wire), and many levels in between. The range of music and their creators defines "eclectic," while the writing veers from freewheeling to acutely insightful. In essence, the books are for the music fan who (as Rolling Stone noted) "thinks liner notes just aren't enough."
—*The Irish Times*

For reviews of individual titles in the series, please visit our blog at 333sound.com and our website at https://www.bloomsbury.com/academic/music-sound-studies/

Follow us on Twitter: @333books

Like us on Facebook: https://www.facebook.com/33.3books
For a complete list of books in this series, see the back of this book.

Forthcoming in the series:

BBC Radiophonic Workshop:
A Retrospective

William L. Weir

BLOOMSBURY ACADEMIC

NEW YORK • LONDON • OXFORD • NEW DELHI • SYDNEY

BLOOMSBURY ACADEMIC
Bloomsbury Publishing Inc
1385 Broadway, New York, NY 10018, USA
50 Bedford Square, London, WC1B 3DP, UK
29 Earlsfort Terrace, Dublin 2, Ireland

BLOOMSBURY, BLOOMSBURY ACADEMIC and the Diana logo are
trademarks of Bloomsbury Publishing Plc

First published in the United States of America 2023

Bloomsbury Publishing Inc does not have any control over, or responsibility
for, any third-party websites referred to or in this book. All internet addresses
given in this book were correct at the time of going to press. The author and
publisher regret any inconvenience caused if addresses have
changed or sites have ceased to exist, but can accept no
responsibility for any such changes.

Whilst every effort has been made to locate copyright holders the publishers
would be grateful to hear from any person(s) not here acknowledged.

A catalog record for this book is available from the Library of Congress.

ISBN: PB: 978-1-5013-8915-3
ePDF: 978-1-5013-8917-7
eBook: 978-1-5013-8916-0

Series: 33 1/3

Typeset by Newgen KnowledgeWorks Pvt. Ltd., Chennai, India
Printed and bound in Great Britain

To find out more about our authors and books visit www.bloomsbury.com
and sign up for our newsletters.

For my wife, Tanya, and son, Lincoln,
who bring me joy every day

Contents

Introduction: An Improbable Stew

In the spring of 1958, the newly opened space in BBC's Maida Vale Studio didn't look like much to anyone who didn't know better: some tape recorders and various gadgets that had been kicking around since the war. Also, some tin cans and a thumb piano made from bicycle spokes.

The sound of the future, it turned out, would come from a roomful of discarded electronics and a box of knickknacks.

Here, a rotating group of employees known as the BBC Radiophonic Workshop would introduce a nation to the strange new world of electronic music. They took the wildest musical innovations of avant-garde composers and repurposed them for news shows, nature documentaries, and children's programs. Freed from their high-art origins, these sounds filled homes, schools, and workplaces, and became the soundtrack of everyday British life. The Workshop would introduce millions of people to sampling, looping, electronic tones, and countless forms of studio magic—the stuff that makes up so much of popular music today. Charged with the relatively modest task of adding some sonic zip to radio and TV shows, it wound up reshaping the sound of the twentieth century.

All this, as one Workshop staffer put it, with little more than "£2,000, one room, a packet of razor blades, and a lot of nerve."[1]

For most of the 1950s, you could hear electronic music only in thorny experimental compositions and horror movie soundtracks. But thanks to the Workshop, these beeps and buzzes, once so jarring and alien, grew familiar to BBC audiences. From there, the Workshop's influence would find its way into psychedelia, glam, synthpop, ambient music, and eventually chart-topping love songs and dance tunes.

While established experimentalist composers worked within the tightly closed loop of academia, the ubiquitous BBC gave the anonymous composers of the Workshop a tremendous reach—millions of people of every age and background heard these sounds every day. No other musicians—not even the Beatles!—could claim that kind of an audience. It created the *Doctor Who* theme, the one everyone knows and has been called the most important piece of electronic music. But the Workshop's influence worked in other, stealthier, ways. Highbrow dramas, news programs, and goofball comedies also made use of electronic sounds. Afternoon talk shows aimed at women featured musique concrète compositions. Through educational programming, schoolchildren took in the radiophonic music that accompanied their reading and math lessons. The impact was huge. The Radiophonic Workshop's work put a permanent stamp on the brains of future musicians, providing them with the first electronic sounds they ever heard. Raised on the BBC, these kids who didn't know what music was "supposed" to sound like, stored these sounds in their mental sonic libraries. They grew up to be the Human League, Portishead, Aphex Twin, Orbital, Prodigy, and many others.

Those who shaped the Workshop over its forty years—Daphne Oram, Desmond Briscoe, Delia Derbyshire, and Brian Hodgson, among them—couldn't foresee the effect that their work would have. How did a ragtag group of engineers, typists, and studio managers have such a massive impact on music? It took a weird stew of improbable elements to make the BBC Radiophonic Workshop possible. These included, but were not limited to: postwar experimentalists, pop music, Samuel Beckett, skiffle, tangled bureaucracy, metal lampshades, and a philosophical clash over the arts and their role in Britain's identity.

A quick survey of the Workshop output reads like a time-lapsed history of pop music's evolution. Its composers made electronic music before there were synthesizers. They hacked into machines to produce entirely new sounds, and used tape loops before almost anyone else. With recorded samples of sound (clanging a piece of metal, say, or the sounds of construction in the neighboring studio), they manipulated the tape to coax out strange, never-before-heard music. They made tunes from door knockers and cash registers. They could turn the wind into a melody and use footsteps as its rhythm. Long before Pro Tools and GarageBand, the Workshop staff collapsed the boundary between composer, performer, and recording engineer. Merging the experimental and the popular, the Workshop erased the line between the high-brow and the low-brow.

Plenty of innovative music came out of the late 1950s. The Workshop, though, made people wonder what "music" itself is. It didn't use conventional instruments, and its compositions could never be recreated live. The Workshop's ways lay so far outside the norm that the BBC refused to classify them as "musicians" at all, deeming its makers "assistants" rather than "composers." For a while, it even limited employees' time at the Workshop, fearing that these sounds—so unlike anything anyone previously knew—would cause psychological distress.

A recurring theme in this book involves the tricky ways that musical influence works and how—with barely anyone noticing—the Workshop deeply affected the culture. Despite its innovation and wide reach, the Workshop and its impact amounted to a kind of secret history. Academics paid attention to electronic music only when it came from one of their own. Mainstream audiences oohed and ahhed when electronics occasionally showed up in pop music. But the sounds that the Workshop piped into homes, schools and work every day? Hidden in plain sight, that was the stuff that truly prepared a nation's ears for the future.

Growing up in America, I had no idea that various English bands I heard on the radio—Roxy Music, say, or Pink Floyd—had drawn heavily from the Workshop's endless well of ideas. It didn't occur to me that something like a jingle for a local radio news program on another continent could, in some form, wend its way into "real" music. The arbitrary ways we decide which music is "real" has a lot to do with that. Even as the Workshop helped steer the larger world of music in a new direction, the cultural gatekeepers paid no attention to TV and radio theme tunes.

The Second World War also plays a big part in the Workshop story. It provided an abundance of oscillators, tape machines and other electronics—and technicians with the know-how to turn them into musical instruments. It also provided the motivation to create this new artform. Bombings and brutality ripped out the foundations of Britain, literally and figuratively. From the wreckage emerged the need for new ways of doing things, including music. A lot of early electronic music arose from attempts to lighten the darkness of the war years.

The war also meant that more women could enter the workplace, including at the BBC. That would prove instrumental for the Workshop, where women were among its most prominent members and did groundbreaking work during an era that offered them few opportunities.

We see, again and again, that everything becomes something else in the Workshop world. Engineers became composers, military communications equipment became music-making machines, and tape recorders became tools for composing. A culture of thriftiness shaped the lean postwar years in England. The same mentality that devised "meat" pies out of carrots would also make futuristic music from dusty, unwanted equipment. Today we call it "DIY" or maybe a "punk rock ethos." Back then, it was just how things got done.

##

Choosing a compilation album falls outside standard 33⅓ practice, but I have my reasons. With 107 tracks over two CDs (don't worry, I'm not going to cover all of them individually), *BBC Radiophonic Workshop: A Retrospective* is the commercial release that best covers the Workshop story. It stretches from its threadbare origins when it took weeks to make a few seconds of music on antique machines, to the era when cutting-edge synthesizers filled its studio.

It's not the best-known of the Workshop's releases. That would be the 1968 self-titled album commonly known as "The Pink Album," which showcases the Workshop's artsier side. But *Retrospective* highlights one of the most interesting things about the Workshop—how its music filled the spaces of a day, often in the background. From wacky *Goon Show* sound effects to the lush soundtracks of nature programs, these tracks—some as short as ten seconds—were the sounds of everyday Britain between 1958 and 1998. That a state-funded organization could generate so much ingenious weirdness remains one of the fascinating things about the Workshop.

Retrospective boasts an impressive range. The early tape music can be atmospheric and haunting or boast a jaunty, steam-punky charm. The later synthesizer-based tracks bear traces of Prog, New Age, and Ambient. With a collection this expansive and covering four decades, you're bound to like certain things more than others. My bias toward the earlier pre-synthesizer music becomes apparent throughout the book. Electronic tones constantly harass our twenty-first-century ears, so they're easy to take for granted. But in 1958—well before synthesizers were effectively available— it took a crazy amount of time to make this music. Made with test oscillators, miles of tape, dense math equations, and deadline-induced desperation—these tracks sound like entire sonic worlds built from the ground up.

The Workshop's composers took electronic music from the cultural fringe and delivered it to living rooms throughout Britain. All the more remarkable is that they did so within a conservative BBC establishment that was often hostile to their efforts. Clad in their neatly pressed office attire, the Workshop members quietly, radically, led a revolution that would change music forever.

1

Before the Workshop: Beeps, Bloops, and a Battle for the Nation's Identity

The sun would be coming up over London soon, and Daphne Oram needed to get moving. The pricey, bulky contraptions had to be back in their rightful places before her coworkers began filing in for work. As always, at the end of her overnight sessions, Oram gathered up the many reel-to-reel tape machines that she commandeered hours earlier and herded them back to their assigned studios.

By the time normal work hours began, no trace would be left of Oram's late-night treks into the outer reaches of mid-twentieth-century music, done well out of sight of her higher-ups in the BBC Music Department. To create the music in her head, Oram needed certain technology. And she could get access to it only by working in the dead of night on the deserted sixth floor of the BBC's Broadcasting House.

When we talk about electronic music today, synthesizers usually spring to mind. But in 1957, they're not even in the picture. The equipment at Oram's disposal was limited to whatever she could scrounge up in the various, temporarily abandoned rooms on the sixth floor after everyone else had gone home. In addition to multiple tape machines, this included oscillators used for acoustics tests or for measuring the response of electrical circuits. They weren't designed to make music. But these devices could produce an audio signal, and early electronic musicians discovered that by turning the dial to change the pitch or by recording and manipulating the signal on tape, they could eke out some interesting sounds. Oscillators would eventually be the thing that gave voice to synthesizers, but at this point, making music with them wasn't easy. To further shape the sound, Oram also built her own audio filters to weed out unwanted frequencies.

When she was seven years old, Oram talked of her ambition to one day build a giant machine that could make any sound she could imagine. That dream never went away. As a studio manager at the BBC Music department, Oram campaigned hard for a studio that could compete with the ones in Paris and Cologne. Those state-funded hotbeds of sonic experimentation had seemingly endless institutional support. She began agitating for it in 1952, and met roadblocks the whole way: fear of the new, lack of resources, internal politics. Being a woman probably didn't help.

In 1956, she submitted a paper to BBC officials, again trying to sell them on creating a world-class experimental music studio: "Once the composer can write without the limitations of performance, his palette is extended enormously," she enthused.[1] No rhythm is too complicated, timbres can be anything you can imagine!

"Miss Oram," one official told her, "the BBC employs a hundred musicians to make all the sounds they require, thank you."[2]

Well, thank *you*, Oram thought, and went ahead anyway. With no encouragement (not a problem for Oram) and no equipment (more of a problem), she got creative. That's how she ended up "borrowing" other departments' tape machines, oscillators, and other equipment at ungodly hours. With these, she would fashion a rig in the Broadcasting House's "absolutely forbidden"[3] 6A Studio for her clandestine experiments. During business hours, the BBC used these state-of-the-art tape machines to play back orchestral concerts, remove the "*uhs*" and "*ums*" from interviews, and other workaday tasks. At night, they became tools for Oram's sonic alchemy. She cut and spliced recorded sounds on tape, changed their speeds, and filtered frequencies. While still learning the capabilities of these machines, and while the rest of the world slept, Oram created sounds that had never been heard before.

"I evolved techniques, akin to Cologne and Paris," she said, "which could be achieved with the normal broadcasting equipment I had available."[4]

These compositions would pave the way for the establishment of the BBC Radiophonic Workshop, which would supply the sounds of Britain for four decades. At the time, though, they stirred a panic among the heads of BBC Music.

Why such hostility toward these new sounds?

After the Second World War, some saw electronic music as a way to make a clean break from a recent past that most people were eager to forget. The war changed Europe's landscape, so why not change the soundscape as well? A new world needed new sounds. Oram was in this camp. Her bosses in the BBC Music Department, though, were in the other. Rather than starting anew, they wanted to rebuild the nation's cherished cultural institutions to their prewar status. Their mission, as one BBC Music official put it, was the "guardianship of rational development of musical aesthetics in this country."[5]

Up to the years following the Second World War, classical music had been king. People either liked it or aspired to like it. But various crazes of the 1950s made it difficult to keep it this way. If it wasn't rock-n-roll teenagers storming the barricades, it was the hep cats of jazz. The greatest threat to this cultural hierarchy, though, came from within the world of classical music. Composers on "the continent"[i] had launched an attack on melody and harmony with serialism, a complex and mostly atonal system of composing that tended to leave audiences cold. Not long after the war, things got even more off-kilter. In Paris and Cologne, the two capitals of musical experimentalism, composers were turning oscillators, turntables, and magnetic recording tape into musical instruments.

As a practical matter, the Musicians' Union frowned on all of this. Radio and records were already eating away at the need for live music; musicians certainly didn't want to

[i] As the rest of Europe is often referred to in the UK.

lose jobs to sine waves and white noise generators. It was also a matter of principle. BBC Music had no intention of allowing pieces of laboratory equipment—*beeping!* and *blooping!* or whatever they do—anywhere near their cellos and glockenspiels. As for what they were doing in Paris and Cologne? "Little beyond freakishness," as one BBC exec put it.[6]

About this Freakishness

Pierre Schaeffer, the figurehead for experimental music in Paris, developed the technique of musique concrete in his studio at the Radiodiffusion-Télévision Française shortly after the war. Recordings of various sounds—trains passing, wind blowing, pretty much anything—became building blocks for his compositions. Fiddle with these sounds enough by changing their speeds, reversing them, or through sheer repetition, and you remove their original associations (you hear a train not as a train, for instance, but as a purely sonic phenomenon).

Composers in Cologne, Germany, the other hub of postwar experimentalism, had even more cause to break from their country's recent past under the Nazis. They insisted on doing everything from scratch. Instead of venturing out into the world to record sounds to mold like clay, they conjured their own tones with oscillators and filters while sealed inside a studio. They called it *elektronische musik*. Both sides had elaborate reasons for why their way was the best. The crux of this dispute—purely electronic sounds versus recorded ones—seemed important at the time. As years went on, though, each incorporated the other's techniques. Boundaries have blurred enough that, today, it all gets categorized as "early electronic music."

Composers at the Paris and Cologne studios had the resources and freedom to go wherever their creative muses took them. Mainstream audiences, though, didn't necessarily follow. Comments like "shockingly unlistenable music" and concerns about jobs for "real" musicians got bandied about on the continent. A 1956 review lamented that Stockhausen's "Gesang Der Jünglinge" treated the human voice "as if it were mud" and poured "hellish sonic pulp"[7] over the audience. And that's his most popular piece! But for the Paris and Cologne composers, this was sticks and stones. Their state-funded studios, impervious to popular opinion, had their backs.

Samuel Beckett and the Theater Inside Your Skull

Oram, who took no side in the Paris-Cologne squabble, was excited by the newness of it all. She wanted to be a part of it, even if that meant toiling away overnight in solitude.

At the BBC, her own Music Department ignored Oram's musical experiments, but kindred spirits in the Drama Department took notice. This included Desmond Briscoe, a studio manager looking to work these new sounds into his radio drama productions. And unlike Oram, Briscoe had the support of his bosses in Drama. She and Briscoe teamed up, giving Oram an end run around the obstructionists in Music. It also allowed skittish BBC officials to sidestep delicate internal politics. They could promote these *zaps* and *whooshes* as the next generation of sound effects—not as "music"—and keep the precarious BBC applecart intact.

Having allies in Drama proved valuable. While the postwar music establishment avoided the new and unfamiliar, theater embraced it. In the 1950s, broadcast radio had only been around for about thirty years. It proved a powerful medium for drama—sets, costumes, and actors' expressions all existed within the imaginations of its audiences. "It is in fact your skull that has become the theater,"[8] as one BBC actor put it.

Radio could reach massive audiences in the intimacy of their own homes. It was perfect for the 1950s' increasingly cerebral theater, and playwrights wanted to make better use of it. Samuel Beckett, of *Waiting for Godot* fame, led the charge.

Beckett had always considered the sound of words when writing. By the 1950s, he was kicking around the idea of radio drama productions that relied as much on sound as on dialogue. The storytelling possibilities of radio stoked his imagination. Done properly, it could bring out the inner lives of his characters in a way that conventional theater couldn't. Maybe the BBC could help with this, he thought.

Eager to push radio drama into the future, BBC Drama department heads jumped at the chance to work with Beckett. It was a smart move. A play by Beckett—who's going to say no to Beckett?—was the perfect Trojan horse to sneak the sounds of musique concrete onto the airwaves.

Beckett's characters tend to be a moody and introspective bunch; the real action takes place internally. If the BBC folks wanted to work with Beckett—and they did, very much—they needed sound effects to convey nervous breakdowns, existential dread, and the full dramatic experience. The old broomstick-hitting-a-rug wouldn't cut it. They needed something ethereal, otherworldly—weirder. They needed radiophonics.

The result was *All that Fall*, Beckett's first play for the BBC, based on characters from his childhood. Beckett wrote in a letter to his friend that the story "full of cartwheels and dragging of feet and puffing and panting"[9] came to him in the dead of night. In charge of the sound effects, Oram's new ally, Desmond Briscoe pulled out all the stops. He used clocks, dripping faucets, and drums to compose spooky footstep sounds in a 4/4 time signature. Then, he played with the speed of the actors' speech and animal sounds to fit the tempo of the footsteps. For rainfall, he huddled employees around a microphone "all going 'tsts tst tssttts tsts' with their lips."[10] A form of tape feedback known as flutter-echo provided a surrealist touch. All these tricks combined to turn the sounds of everyday life into music.

Although they put their own stamp on it, Briscoe and the BBC took direction from Beckett, who stayed current on wireless and recording technologies and paid attention to the power of sound. He wrote audio cues into his script, even distinguishing between "silence" and "pause."[11]

The radio play went over like gangbusters. Critics loved the otherworldly score, calling it "a miraculous web of sound effects," and "a feather in the cap for sound drama."[12] Beckett himself was pleased by the production, if a little annoyed at the choice to use humans to make the animal sounds. Real cows don't moo in rhythm, Briscoe explained.

A lot was riding on the production, so this was big. High on success, Oram and Briscoe worked with Drama to hatch out more plans for these new-fangled sounds. Later that year, Oram produced the sounds for *Private Dreams and Public Nightmares*, a short play by Frederick Bradnum. The BBC advertised it as "a radiophonic poem," using that term publicly for the first time.

The Barricades Come Down

Besides Beckett and his fellow playwrights, reinforcements to the pro-radiophonics faction arrived from the other end of the cultural spectrum: Wildly popular comedian Spike Milligan and his madcap *Goon Show* pals saw in radiophonics a new world of kooky sound effects. The barricades would hold only so much longer. In 1957, the BBC took the very tentative step of designating Oram as the BBC's one-person "Radiophonic Unit" ("Electrophonic," the first choice for the name, had associations with hearing and brain research). The new position provided Oram with an office and exactly one tape recorder. But the high demand for weird sounds prompted the BBC to soon elevate the "Radiophonic Unit" to a "Radiophonic Workshop." It officially opened on April 1, 1958, with thirty-two-year-old Oram as its first studio manager and a small staff that included Briscoe. Making clear the Workshop's mission, Oram posted a copy of *New Atlantis* on one of the studio's walls. Francis Bacon's seventeenth-century Utopian tale describes "artificial echoes," and "sound-houses" that "demonstrate all sounds and their generation." Oram read it as an early foretelling of electronic music.

The day it opened, the BBC declared the Workshop "the first installation of its kind in this country," providing a kind of sound for radio and TV productions that "neither music nor conventional sound effects can give." The *Times of London* called it a place for "producing synthetic sound, partly by electronic oscillators and partly by trickery with conventional sounds recorded on tape."

Supplementing their tiny budget, the staff had their run of the Redundant Plant, the BBC's equipment graveyard, to scavenge whatever the more affluent departments had tossed out—mostly things cloaked in years of dust. Between the money and storage room raids, they had some oscillators and tape machines that ran at different speeds. From the nearby Royal Albert Hall, they acquired a 1943 sound mixer that had once crashed to the floor from a great distance. They had boxes of gravel and other noisemakers. It was a far cry from Oram's vision of the UK's most advanced music studio.

"We didn't have much equipment—we were mostly using a three-tape recorder technique," Oram said. "And one oscillator. We had one filter—it was a great day when the filter arrived!"[13]

"Radiophonic" sounds like a hokey space-age coinage typical for the 1950s, but the term had been around for a while. Evoking images of shiny circuits and bolts of electricity, the BBC used it loosely for any sounds produced electronically or with tape manipulation. The term "Workshop" has its roots in drama. "Laboratory" would have been more accurate, but "Workshop" gives a certain down-to-earth feel to something that probably seemed pretty flighty at that time. Overall, "Radiophonic Workshop" neatly combines the everyday and a 1950s idea of "futuristic."

On its first day, though, the Workshop's studio didn't look like the future of anything. It was housed in Rooms 13 and 14 of London's Maida Vale Studios, about two miles from BBC's headquarters. Built in the baroque/art nouveau style in 1909, the former 2,650-person-capacity Maida Vale Roller Skating Palace and Club was Europe's largest skating rink—too big, it turns out. Construction began at the height of the roller-skating boom, and finished just as the craze had fizzled out. It closed in three months.[14] The BBC bought it in 1932, retaining its "Victorian railway station"[15] style and decorative stucco arches at each entrance. The rink's spectator gallery would become the Workshop's first rooms. The BBC's symphony and chamber groups set up shop and various rock bands performed live broadcasts there. Otherwise, it was a lot like any other workplace—offices, harried employees, and internal politics. Some days, though, you might see someone like Muhammad Ali, or conductor Leopold Stokowski in the cafeteria. Maybe even both at the same table.

The first track on *Retrospective* is part of the BBC's first wholly electronic score for a television show, for a production of the play *Amphitryon 38*. Oram created it with a sine wave oscillator, a tape recorder, and filters that she made herself. The fifty-second snippet offered on *Retrospective* is the only bit that survives. The first half of the track has a wavering high pitch floating over a bed of rumbling hiss. Toward the end, the rumbling takes precedence. A rapid series of tinny percussive sounds makes a final flourish before silence.

Disconnected from the play's story of Greek gods, the short bit of music evokes a time when electricity still held a certain spooky mystery.

This and other sounds produced in the early days of the Workshop really don't sound much different from what the Cologne and Paris studios were producing. In retrospect, the whole "sound effects vs. music" debate didn't amount to much. But these distinctions mattered at the time. Even as they announced the opening of the Workshop, BBC officials clarified that radiophonics is "not an art in itself."

There were other trade-offs. Afraid of the mental health effects of electronic sounds, the BBC limited employee assignments to the Workshop to three months. After that, they rotated to other, presumably less psychologically taxing, assignments. This sounds like the kind of goofy workplace lore passed from one generation of employees to the next. But it checks out; there really was such a policy. It didn't last long, and its origins are murky. Former Workshop director Brian Hodgson blames it on a doctor friend of someone high up in the BBC chain: "They didn't want any loonies on their staff." The policy's exact nature is unclear—some say it was for three months, others say six. Also, there seems to be some inconsistency as to who was subject to the rule.

It sounds silly today, as our cell phones buzz and dishwashers continually beep out tunes, but who in the 1950s could say for sure that these sounds—which appear nowhere in the natural world—wouldn't scramble brains and drive people bonkers? Besides, Hodgson said with a laugh, "he was probably right."

Anonymity also came with the deal; even when employees completed a piece from beginning to end entirely by themselves, collective credit went to the Radiophonic Workshop.

At least the BBC finally recognized that making sound with tape manipulation and electronics could be a vital craft. Not an art, of course, as the BBC made clear. For now, Oram would take what she could get. She'd gotten this far through years of working late hours and striking unlikely alliances. From here, Oram figured she could shape the Workshop into that giant machine of infinite sounds she dreamed of.

Troubles lay ahead for Oram, but on April 1, 1958, that was some way off. The BBC Radiophonic Workshop had officially opened, and in its own weird, ramshackle way, it represented the future. And it looked fantastic.

2

"Vive Le Workshop!"

When Current Exceeds Capacity

As a teenager, Daphne Oram would alter the sounds of her parents' piano by wedging metal clips and wads of paper between the strings (this would have been right around the time that American composer John Cage introduced the prepared piano). Both tech-savvy and mischievous, she'd then broadcast these spooky sounds to other parts of her house to scare her parents and their guests. She pulled off these pranks with early wireless technology that she and her brothers devised with equipment from the First World War.[1]

Growing up in rural Wiltshire, England, the connections between music and electronics fascinated Oram. She was hardly alone in this. For centuries, the possibility that electricity and its many applications somehow intermingled with the spiritual and metaphysical worlds had enthralled many. Folks in the eighteenth century considered lightning a sign of God's wrath (some nations feared Ben Franklin's ability to harness it, afraid that he might deploy some kind of death ray on his enemies). Guglielmo Marconi tried fashioning his wireless technology to tap into the universe's sound waves and hear Jesus Christ's last words. Relative to human history, this technology was still new by the time Oram became aware of it. It took the world some time to adjust. Meanwhile, the voices spilling from the crackles and squeals of radio speakers seemed like magic.

A tired complaint about electronic music (and one you still hear today) is that it's cold and emotionless. But electronic systems and the sounds they could produce gave Oram the language to describe life. Her writings on electronic music reveal a soulful worldview that saw capacitors, filters, and ring modulators as a window into the human experience.

"Is this an analogy for life?" she writes of frequency wave patterns in her 1972 book, *An Individual Note*, a loosely structured treatise on music, electronics, and life. "Do we ever perceive reality? Is reality always disguised—always an indecipherable intermodulation between ourselves and 'what lies beyond'?" Maybe St. Peter had something similar in mind, Oram wonders, when he declared that "the world was created by the word of God so that what is seen is made out of things that do not appear."

In photos, Oram's ever-present 1950s-style librarian glasses and tidy appearance belie a wild, inventive, and far-reaching mind. Oram possessed a curiosity that steered her toward not just music and electronics, but into archeology, the Bible, spirituality, psychic phenomena, Eastern philosophy, acupuncture, and so much more—all of which she somehow threaded together into a worldview unlike any other. On paper, her wonky electrical engineering expertise mixed with New Age woo-woo suggests a person who might be difficult company. But apparently not. She had lots of friends and by all accounts, was an eager and cheerful mentor to aspiring tape music composers.

Oram's niece, Carolyn Scales, remembers her as a doting aunt, but also as someone eager to trade "ideas, ideas, ideas" with Scales' equally tech-obsessed father.

"You go in the door, and she was absolutely delighted to see us—great hugs and things," she said. "She'd say 'Oh, come and have your cup of tea,' but she was already on—'I've just been thinking of this idea and that idea.' That's what came out—this incredible … I don't know, just thoughts, thoughts, thoughts."

Oram once traveled to Trinidad and Tobago to work on a film project. She befriended her driver, who invited Oram to his niece's Hindu wedding ceremony. She made an audio recording of it (because that's what she did). While recording traffic sounds the following day, she met a family on the side of the road. *They* invited her to their sugarcane farm, where she recorded the cutting and slashing of the crop. And the *next* day, she convinced a police brass band to let her record their performance.[2] This sequence of events perfectly highlights how sound—the thing that drove Oram in every way—brought her to new places and experiences. It connected her to new people, who in turn, embraced this bespectacled stranger traipsing through a tropical island with her bulky Nagra reel-to-reel tape machine in tow.

Her parents initially discouraged her music ambitions, steering her toward a career in electrotherapy. In 1942, though, her family held a seance at their home (not that odd for the time, actually—spiritualism was fairly popular in 1940s' England). The medium Leslie Flint, who later gained fame as a huckster psychic, told Oram that the spirit of a great musician would assist her. And with that, her parents relented.

She joined the BBC that year at age seventeen. The war-induced shortage of employable men gave female employees new opportunities to work their way up. For an early assignment as a music department studio assistant, she stood ready during live music broadcasts with a concert recording in her hands. If bombs should fall on London, she could immediately cue up the disc to keep the music going uninterrupted for listeners at home.

But she had bigger ideas. In 1948—about the time of the first musical experiments in Paris and Cologne—she composed *Still Point*, a piece for double orchestra, five microphones, and three turntables. It's possibly the first composition to combine live electronic manipulation with acoustic orchestration. The BBC rejected Oram's request to have it performed.

Back to the Workshop: "Everyone's Learned about Us!"

Weeks after it opened, the Workshop took on James Hanley's radio drama *The Ocean*. It tells a grim story of five men, including an old priest, stranded on a lifeboat after their ship has been torpedoed. The main theme of the play is the second track on *Retrospective*, and is a group effort by Oram, Briscoe, and engineer Richard "Dickie" Bird.

As they did with *All that Fall*, the production blurs the point where natural sounds become music and vice versa. A clarinet and some water sloshing in a washbasin provide the sound sources, but tape manipulation gives it an inside-your-head claustrophobic feel. It suits the characters' internal monologues. Briscoe said they wanted to convey the crushing monotony of being stranded on the ocean. The low tones, wavering up and down, remind me of both waves and the foghorn of a barge. It all comes together in such a way that the sixty-seven-second track just crosses the line from sound effects over to music, and then back again.

It introduces the Workshop with a flourish. It's musical (kind of), and the sounds seem to come from real, physical objects (again, kind of, and in a way that you can't be sure what those objects might be). It also sticks to the Paris school of experimentalism, opting for the softer and more natural sounds of musique concrete rather than the harsher electronic tones of Cologne. Overall, the track ("The Ocean" No. 2 on Disc 1) showcases Oram's knack for "getting things down to its absolute simplicity," as described by longtime Workshop member Dick Mills.

"You want loneliness and an empty ocean? Here's a washing-up bowl and a clarinet. Get on with it."[3]

One reviewer described the sounds as a "groaning dirge of some inhuman voice." He meant that in a good way, but it echoed Briscoe's concerns that the Workshop's output tended toward the gloomier side of things. According to Mills, audience feedback included phrases like "fearful noise" and "it sounds like skeletons on a corrugated iron roof."

Fearful noise or not, the Workshop sounds got attention, and producers wanted more. "They got to know about it, the various departments, and they all rushed at us and we had so much work," Oram said. "I wrote a letter that I sent to my mother, saying 'I can't write any more letters because there's so much work coming in—everyone's learned about us!' "[4]

The Workshop Cares if You Listen

Breaking from the onslaught of score requests, Oram joined some fellow BBC employees on a field trip to the Brussels World Fair in October 1958 to witness the "Journées Internationales de Musique Expérimentale"—a week of experimental music. A Pierre Schaeffer lecture kicked off a concert of musique concrete performances. Edgard Varese's *Poeme Electronique* debuted on a massive and complex loudspeaker system inside the Philips Pavilion, a structure that iconic architect Le Corbusier modeled after the human stomach ("It should appear as though you are about to enter a slaughterhouse,"[5] he instructed). Architect/composer Iannis Xenakis did most of the heavy design work on the building and contributed the short composition *Concret PH*, made with the sounds of burning charcoal.

A little like the Sex Pistols' famous Manchester show—in which nearly everyone in attendance went on to shape music in some way—the audience at the Brussels event proved as significant as the music itself. If you were a mid-century maker of experimental music, or aspired to be one, it's a good bet that you visited the World Fair in October of 1958.

Up-and-comers like future Workshop collaborator Tristram Cary and Denmark's Else Marie Pade were there. Four years before she would join the Workshop, Delia Derbyshire attended. The event had a particular impact on Derbyshire, who would later paraphrase Varese to defend the Workshop's output: "It was music, it was abstract electronic sound, organized."[6] Future Kraftwerk member Ralf Hutter, twelve years old at that time, attended with his parents in tow. Big names like Luciano Berio, Karlheinz Stockhausen, Bruno Maderna, Henri Pousseur, Marina Scriabine, and Luc Ferrari were also there, either lecturing, performing, or just lending support. There's a photo of all of them, with John Cage lying down and the others hamming it up for the camera—any bad blood between Paris and Cologne apparently water under the bridge.

Oram's fellow BBC delegates left Brussels unimpressed. One BBC official scoffed at Stockhausen and the other composers' impractical methods and the "much too loud and noisy" sounds they produced. "*Vive Le Workshop!*"[7] he wrote in his report.

Oram, on the other hand, returned from Brussels fired up. Fascinated by what she heard and saw, the event only fueled her resolve to get the Workshop the kind of creative freedom that the Paris and Cologne studios enjoyed. She wanted a space to welcome world-class composers, and create music for its own sake—not just to accompany programs. But the BBC didn't budge. The Music Department still showed no interest in electronic music, and the Workshop's assignments came almost exclusively from Drama and Features. Demand from programming was too high. Who had time for highfalutin stand-alone projects? Besides, they reminded Oram, there's still the three-months-or-you'll-go-crazy policy: You'll be reassigned soon.

A lot of things took their toll on Oram at this time and to look over notes in her archive, you can easily get lost in the weeds of it all. She wanted modern music to have its own place in the culture, and not just as "imaginative background to drama productions," as the BBC once put it. In her book, Oram draws an analogy that sums up her plight with the BBC: Her ambition—the electrical circuit—exceeded the capacity of the BBC system, resulting in distortion. As in music, some distortion in life can make things interesting. But at some point, it gets to be too much.

Oram would later put much of the blame on Donald McWhinnie, Head of Drama at the time. Like Briscoe and Oram, McWhinnie kept up with the latest in experimental music. And without his support in the face of the Music department's interference, the Workshop probably never would have happened. It also meant, though, that Oram had to work with Drama, a compromise that she felt reduced the Workshop to a sound effects factory. "What a pity he interfered!"[8] she would write years later.

It's hard not to root for Oram with all her pluck and single-mindedness. We're conditioned to side with the visionary artist facing down the clueless suits. But sometimes management and the bean counters have a point. What if her vision won out, and the Workshop didn't need to worry about mainstream audiences? It's hard to believe that this alternate universe Workshop would have had the same impact on music.

Two months before the Workshop officially opened, *High Fidelity* magazine published electronic composer Milton Babbitt's essay "Who Cares If You Listen?" Babbitt argued that "advanced music" doesn't need popular listenership: "After all, the public does have its own music," he wrote. Instead of chasing after audiences, he counsels composers to take a "total, resolute and voluntary withdrawal from this public world to one of private performance."[9] But the Workshop showed that the public could appreciate these sounds— the trick was in how they were presented. The Workshop cared deeply that you listened—the whole operation depended on it. Existing entirely outside the lowbrow-to-highbrow spectrum, the Workshop snuck the rarely heard experimental sounds of Paris and Cologne into millions of homes.

What if you could go back to that winter of 1959 to convince Oram to see things differently, that the Workshop would forge its own identity to become a genuine cultural force? It wouldn't have mattered. By this point, Oram had a mission. Within a year she would become the first woman with her own electronic music studio, housed in an old, conical oasthouse (once used to dry hops for making beer) that looked like something out of a Hans Christian Andersen tale. Within two years, she would compose *Four Aspects*, a piece that anticipated the music of Brian Eno. She would also pioneer her "drawn sound" technique, Oramics, inspired by an "artificial talker" machine she saw on a BBC program.

Oramics never really took off, and things in general didn't work out quite as she'd hoped. Much of her income would come from composing ad music for Anacin, Nestea, and others (much of which was also brilliant). But she never gave up on her life's work, which she described as the "study of sound in its relationship to life." In any case, her plans didn't include sticking around the BBC to take orders from Drama. She handed in her resignation in January 1959.

3

"Time Beat" and the Soul of a Machine

Pioneering Automated Rhythm, with no Apologies

For millennia, the rhythms of our bodies—heartbeat, breath, footsteps—set the pace for music. This makes sense—science tells us that we connect most to tunes with tempos similar to the average adult heart rate. First-aid classes famously use "Stayin' Alive" to guide the rate of heart compressions. But starting in the nineteenth century, various technologies—first metronomes, and then tape loops, drum machines, and click tracks—increasingly took over. Essentially, we've outsourced the job of our own biological beat keepers to machinery.

That's a huge philosophical shift about the nature of music, and one that has made entire genres possible—synthpop, disco, and electronica among them. But the human pulse didn't give way to the Roland TR-808 overnight. Of the many things that happened along the way, one very unlikely point in this timeline involves the Workshop, a former typist, and a televised political debate. It's the improbable origin story of an early electronic dance tune that pioneered automated rhythm and proudly put its machine-like properties front and center.

After arriving at the Workshop, fresh from assisting Olympics news coverage in Italy, Maddalena Fagandini quickly became the Workshop's go-to for composing interval signals. These short bits of sound, each unique to the radio or TV station, filled the space between programs. They let audiences know that, yes, the station was active. And like vendors at a flea market, interval signals competed for audience attention against other frequencies on the dial. They usually reflected the country's identity in some way. Radio Australia used "Waltzing Matilda," Swiss Radio International featured a music box, and "Yankee Doodle Dandy" served as Voice of America's interval signal. They added to the medley of functional human-made sounds, like dial tones and ticking clocks, that make up the melodies and rhythms in the background of everyday life.

Fagandini used tape loops to make simple but engaging rhythms. Aiming to grab anyone passing by a radio or TV, short and catchy was key. Impressed, producers assigned Fagandini to compose music for the broadcast of a political debate. She created a sparse rhythm track bearing the profoundly unpromising title "Music for Party Political Conferences."[1] The BBC recycled it for use as an interval signal in 1961.

Listed as "Time Beat" on *Retrospective*, the thirty-one-second track of looped percussion sounds—a combination of clicks, woodblock sounds, and a rubbery bass—ended up as the basis for a more elaborately arranged tune of the same name. It was commercially released as a single in 1962 under the guise of an artist named Ray Cathode.

"I am not Ray Cathode," Fagandini said, laughing, in the BBC documentary *Alchemists of Sound*. "Ray Cathode was a concoction." Fagandini created the rhythm and "then somebody decided they could make a pop record out of it."[2] That somebody was George Martin, not long before gaining fame as producer for the Beatles.

Martin brought a sense of musical adventure to Parlophone, the record label and EMI subsidiary that hired him in 1950. Still itching to try new things ten years later and frustrated by electronic limitations at the Abbey Road studio, Martin paid a visit to the Workshop, about a mile away. There, as he describes it, they were "cooking up freaky sounds, with whatever they could lay their hands on."[3]

After hearing Fagandini's jaunty interval signal, Martin got to thinking and convinced EMI to acquire the rights. He then had studio musicians bring a Latin flair to Fagandini's rhythm track. In retrospect, a Martin-Workshop matchup seems perfect; both were in the business of pushing music's boundaries without pushing away mainstream audiences. The Workshop staff fascinated Martin with how they "flew by the seat of their pants. Everything had to be made laboriously by hand, but it was a labor of love."[4]

The single's B-side, "Waltz in Orbit" (remember, this was the height of space-age fascination), reversed the roles. Martin supplied the rhythm backing and Fagandini conjured a bouncy and buzzy top layer that couples well with a melancholic piano. Both tracks are fun, portraying a rickety version of "the future," like Jetsons-style robots dancing. *Retrospective* includes only Fagandini's original version, but with various reissues, the Martin-ized version and its B-side are readily available.

The BBC policy of anonymity for Workshop employees meant that Fagandini was nowhere in sight when it came to promoting the single. That put all the attention on Martin, and he had a field day with it. He came up with the pseudonym "Ray Cathode" and posed for photos with a computer (supposedly Ray Cathode himself) for the New Musical Express ("Electronic Sounds" was the headline). He told Disc magazine that while musique concrete wasn't new, it was new for pop records. "It is concrete music reinforced by musicians—so we're calling it 'reinforced concrete music.'"[5]

"Time Beat" got a fair amount of radio time, especially on the BBC Light Programme. Overall, it did OK business, but nothing to make anyone call for more Martin-Workshop collaborations. The weirdly punctuated ads for the single— "Here it is at last—electronic 'music'!"—probably didn't help. It may have been the sound of the future, but it definitely wasn't the sound of April 22, 1962, when a judges' panel that included Neil Sedaka deemed it a "miss" on the weekly TV show *Juke Box Jury* (all but one of the other nine songs were "hits").

Even before George Martin worked his magic, Fagandini's original rhythm track—the one for jauntily introducing politicians—breaks from the Workshop's style up to that point. Another Fagandini track, generically titled "Interval

Signal" (*track 10, disc 1*), features looped rhythms layered over each other to become more complex. They peel away to something simpler, and then build back up again. It's closer to earlier percussion-heavy pieces like Edgard Varese's *Ionisation* from 1929. "Time Beat," though, signals the future by marrying the experimental with pop. It's the first track on *Retrospective* with an obvious danceability to it. That's not a small thing, since one of electronic music's biggest contributions to humanity is in all the ways people can dance to it. The track also establishes what would be a recurring theme with the Workshop: the closer it veered to pop, the more revolutionary it was.

Calling it "a landmark of its kind," Briscoe was happy with the Workshop's early venture into the world of pop music, noting that it "created a considerable amount of interest in what the Workshop was doing."[6]

"My Blood and a Mechanical Instrument"

Briscoe was right about it being a landmark. Even if the single didn't fly off the shelves, the fact that Parlophone released it as a pop record at all is a big deal for a song that—at this point in music history—uses a tape loop rhythm. Even among the more adventurous pop musicians, automated rhythm didn't show up much in commercial music. Is it the first electronic dance track, as some claim? Well, it is a dance tune that uses electronic sounds. You probably wouldn't call it electronica, the same way you wouldn't call Blue Cheer the first heavy metal band—they get close to the finish line, but

BBC RADIOPHONIC WORKSHOP: A RETROSPECTIVE

don't quite cross it. But it's close enough to earn its place in music history.

Electronics start making their first appearances—few and far between—in pop music at this time. Del Shannon's 1961 hit "Runaway," for instance, uses a homemade electronic instrument keyboard called the Musitron. But the automated rhythm of "Time Beat"/"Waltz in Orbit" puts it in a different class of sonic pioneers. Even the Tornados' space-age hit "Telstar," written and produced by electronics wiz Joe Meek and released a few months after "Time Beat," featured the flesh and blood Clem Cattini on drums.

Automated rhythm took a while to catch on in the mainstream, but it has long fascinated inventive minds— as early as the fifteenth century, Da Vinci imagined a mechanical drum. Commercially produced drum machines, though, didn't show up until the mid-twentieth century. The Chamberlin Rhythmate, made in 1949, provided percussion sounds with tape loops. In 1959—one year before Fagandini made "Time Beat"—the Wurlitzer Sideman hit stores. Neither machine got far beyond the homes of hobbyists. But the Sideman's promise to let users "hold the whole band in your hand" (distantly predicting the one-person music productions so common in the twenty-first century) rattled musicians' unions at a time of dwindling gigs. It turns out, though, that these drum machines were no threat to the working drummer. In fact, the modern drum kit setup reduced more percussionists' jobs than any machinery. Before the twentieth century, a different musician was assigned to each component of percussion—that is, one person on cymbals, another on the bass drum, and so on.

38

The switch to automated rhythm is a major turning point in the history of music. Thanks to the metronome, we measure tempos today with beats per minute, or BPM. That's a lot more precise than "adagio" (literally, "at ease") or "andante" ("at a walking pace")—the old way of dictating tempo. Even top-notch drummers now occasionally take orders from the click track, essentially an electronic metronome played through headphones: "I have to swallow my pride and be a little subservient to the machine," Rush's Neil Peart admitted.[7]

Of course, not everyone's a fan; the metronome raised some hackles right from the start. Johannes Brahms declared in 1880 that he "never believed that my blood and a mechanical instrument go well together."[8] Composer Daniel Gregory Mason warned in 1909 of the "dangerous" metronome: "Mathematical exactitude gives us a dead body in place of the living musical organism with its ebb and flow of rhythmical energy."[9] The same year, composer Ignacy Jan Paderewski wrote that following a machine in music "means about as much as being sentimental in engineering."[10]

The Workshop, founded on the idea of combining music and engineering, would open nearly a half-century later.

"Stayin' Alive," Back Again

That "Time Beat" is an early (the earliest? It's hard to say) use of automated rhythm on a commercially released pop song is only part of what makes it interesting. The real story is that the song's makers *want you to know* that the snappy beat comes from a nonhuman. It's the difference between convenience and artistic choice.

Exactly where automated rhythm first shows up in pop music is a slippery matter, riddled with all sorts of qualifiers. And if you declare anything a "first" in music, you're looking for a fight. In the Netherlands, Tom Dissevelt and Dick Raaijmakers were making somewhat poppy electronic sounds around this time. But "poppy" is subjective and, technically, you can dance to anything.

"Cathy's Clown," which the Everly Brothers released in 1960, features a tape loop that doubles Buddy Harmon's percussion. It's designed, though, to trick you into thinking that two human drummers are playing. The "Time Beat/Waltz in Orbit" single is a very different thing: the mechanistic, nonhuman quality of the loop is the whole point. Just as Cher's "Believe" played up the robotic splendor of Auto-Tune three decades later, the charm and innovation of "Time Beat" comes from how fake it sounds. Unlike "Cathy's Clown," "Time Beat" not only let a machine take over the rhythm, they let it *sound like* a machine. That puts it way ahead of its time.

It took more than a decade after "Time Beat" for drum machines to show up regularly in pop songs. Even then, they did so with an air of embarrassed secrecy about them. Robin Gibb uses a drum machine on his 1970 solo album, *Robin's Reign*, but it's apologetically buried in the mix. The drum machine's next star turn was on Sly and the Family Stone's 1971 *There's a Riot Goin' On*. Recording the album came during a rough period for Stone, when he had alienated many in his circle. This included human drummers. The "funk box" as he called it, though, was still available. He used it because he ran out of options, and frankly, didn't care that much. But it sounds great. And, crucially, not at all like a human. But still, no one noticed. Unlike George Martin, Stone didn't pose with a computer for publicity photos (a recluse at this point, Stone wasn't posing with anyone). Plus, listeners just didn't know about this stuff. To twenty-first-century ears, it's hard to believe anyone would mistake Stone's drum machine, a Maestro Rhythm King, for a human. Then again, the special effects of 1950s monster movies that seem silly to us now frightened audiences who didn't know any better. "The deal is, in those days people didn't know about it, so they didn't realize what it was," said J. J. Cale, who used a drum machine for his 1971 album *Naturally*.[11]

A few years later, Robin Gibb shows up again in the chronicles of nonhuman drumming, this time with brothers Barry and Maurice, for the Bee Gees' "Stayin Alive." As with Sly Stone, it happened out of desperation—they couldn't get a good groove with traditional drumming. Their engineer, Albhy Galuten, sampled a bar of drums from "Night Fever" and fashioned a tape loop out of it. It produced the perfect mix of machine and human. "The loop crossed the boundary, giving us music that was in time with a good feel,"[12] Galuten said. They *really* liked it—you hear the same tape loop on "More than a Woman," also for the 1977 *Saturday Night Fever* soundtrack, as well as on Barbra Streisand's "Woman in Love."

"Stayin' Alive" gave the world its first chart-topping drum loop. Again, this went pretty much unnoticed by the general public. Even with Galuten calling it a "watershed event in our life and times," the Bee Gees did little to call attention to it. As a nice inside joke, though, they did credit the drums to a "Bernard Lupe," continuing the tradition of personifying nonhuman drums that "Ray Cathode" started.

"We received an unbelievable amount of calls looking for this steady drummer named Bernard Lupe," said coproducer and engineer Karl Richardson. "You know—'This guy's a rock! I've never heard anyone so steady in my life!'"[13]

Two years after "Stayin' Alive," the fastidious duo of Steely Dan credited their customized drum machine as "Wendel" in the liner notes of their album *Gaucho*. Steely Dan's engineer Roger Nichols designed and built it for $150,000, with the goal of ensuring that no one who heard it would be able to tell that it was a machine. When the album was awarded a Grammy, "Wendel" was listed among the winners.

It wasn't until the 1980s that musicians truly embraced the robotic timekeeping of machine-based drums and all their shiny futurism. You can hear the gleeful embrace of artificial beat-keeping on the Human League's 1981 "Don't You Want Me," the first big hit to feature the revolutionary Linn LM-1 drum machine, made available one year earlier. The hypnotic and unfailing beat provides the perfect contrast to the song's all-too-human tale of a bitter breakup. Roger Linn, the machine's inventor, hated "Don't You Want Me." Specifically, he hated the band's choice to program "a very rigid, robotic part"[14] and ignore the features he created to "humanize" the sound. As with Auto-Tune, though, it turned out that "perfecting" human performance was a lot less interesting than letting the machines simply be machines. And Linn's protests didn't stop the device's many subsequent users, like Gary Numan, from also playing up the "machine" part of drum machines.

So why, two decades after "Time Beat," was automated rhythm embraced not just for its reliability but its artificiality? And by British musicians in particular?

When we connect the dots, it all makes sense. Several synthpop bands, whose members had grown up in England with "Time Beat," and other Workshop sounds, happily abandoned human drummers—and didn't care who knew. But the Bee Gees, Roger Linn, and Steely Dan all grew up outside of Britain, their musical instincts unformed by BBC programming. Even among the most independent thinkers, geography plays a big role in how we think about music. In 1984, Prince used the LM-1 drum machine on "When Doves Cry." A voracious and eclectic listener, Prince surely heard the machine's use in British synthpop in the years leading up to *Purple Rain*, and put his own ingenious stamp on it. But Minnesota-born Prince, forward-thinking in so many other ways, showed a conservative streak when it came to presenting the machines in his music. For the video for "When Doves Cry," his Purple Majesty had human drummer Bobby Z. mime the sounds of the LM-1 drum machine.

##

Despite Ray Cathode's short musical career, the ever-optimistic Martin called it "something to learn from anyway!" And learn from it he did. Martin would have his first recording session with the Beatles less than two months after the release of "Time Beat." Teaming with the Workshop, he said, inspired him to try things in Beatles productions that were still new to pop music at that point, like varispeed piano and backward vocals.

For her part, it doesn't appear that being the "godmother of electronic dance music" was something Fagandini gave much thought. Shortly after she died in 2011, her friend and collaborator Giles Oakley said that most people who knew Fagandini weren't even aware of her role in "Time Beat." Fagandini didn't stay at the Workshop long after the single's release. She came to the BBC as a typist and parlayed that entry into a varied career that showcased her eclectic interests, including her production of a Mediterranean cooking show and "The Devil's Music," a documentary on the history of the blues. Briscoe, who called her "a lady of considerable talent and spirit,"[15] said Fagandini was often pulled away from her Workshop duties for other BBC projects that called on her multilingual skills. Eventually, this led to her full-time position as a television producer who innovated a number of foreign language teaching series.

4

Way Out and Catchy! *Doctor Who*, and a New Era for the Workshop

Riding through London on her twenty-year-old bicycle while mentally mapping out her latest compositions, Delia Derbyshire would sing her works-in-progress out loud. Lost in her own music, she would occasionally get lost for real, having wandered from her route to find herself in a strange part of the city.

That was fine; London was a great place. This wasn't the city that the Great Smog swallowed up several years earlier in 1952, choking out thousands of lives and setting the tone for the decade's remainder: inhabitants dressed in various grays, bleak cinema, bleak art. Derbyshire's London was the one of the 1960s, of color photography and fabulous fashions. Flocks of young people, untroubled by war or economic woes, reinvigorated the city. Among these bright and creative folks, Derbyshire and her arrival marked a new era for the Workshop. Soon, the eerie sounds of Beckettian drama gave way to something brighter and catchier. This is the era that produced the Workshop's flagship work, the *Doctor Who* theme.

Doctor Who, the time-traveling series, has proven remarkably resilient. Even more resilient is its theme music, the thing that best connects the current show to its 1963 incarnation. Swooping, hissing, and pulsing with electronic verve, it manages at once to be haunting, goofy, and ethereal. It's a warbling classic of TV music and is probably the thing most responsible for introducing a wide audience to electronic music.

"I want a new sound—way out and catchy!"[1]

That's twenty-eight-year-old dynamo producer, Verity Lambert, barging into the Workshop. The BBC's youngest producer at the time, Lambert previously displayed her sharp instincts as a production assistant for *Armchair Theatre*: Her on-the-fly camera directions kept viewers at home blissfully unaware that a cast member had suffered a fatal heart attack during a live broadcast.

Now she needed a theme for something called *Doctor Who*, aimed at eleven-to-fourteen-year-olds, expected to run six weeks. Specifically, she wanted something "familiar, but different." The Radiophonic Workshop wasn't her first choice. She wanted Les Structures Sonores, a French musical duo who played glass instruments. Their music was haunting, but too pricey for a kids' show with ramshackle cardboard sets. Briscoe suggested composer Ron Grainer, a previous Workshop collaborator. Grainer scrawled out a one-page score, handed it off, and headed off for vacation.

Workshop newbie Derbyshire was tapped to turn the score into actual music—a sign of confidence so early in her tenure.

Also, perhaps, a sign of the low expectations for the show itself. Still, even low-budget TV was big. In just a few years, television sets had gone from luxury items to must-haves. By 1960, three-quarters of the homes in Britain had one. The Workshop's assignments reflected this; the bulk of its workload had shifted from radio productions to television by the early 1960s.

Lambert wanted something that would jump out of the tiny speakers of black-and-white TV sets, and pull people from their kitchens to their living rooms. Familiar but different, way out and catchy. Ethereal musique concrète—still the Workshop's bread and butter—wouldn't cut it. At this point, the Workshop reserved purely electronic tones—too unreliable, too screechy—for special effects. But that changed, with the arrival of both Derbyshire and more oscillators, most of which went to the brand-new Room 12—"Delia's room," as they called it. With a keyboard ripped from an old piano, they now had a custom-built controller—the "Keying Unit"—that made playing a full octave on a set of twelve oscillators a little more intuitive. But it took more than a Rube Goldberg-type device to explain Derbyshire's uncanny flair for coaxing pretty sounds from laboratory equipment.

Music, Math, and "Her Own Complete Language"

Derbyshire came to the Workshop armed with a Cambridge degree in mathematics and music.

"[It was] quite something for a working-class girl in the '50s, and where only one in 10 were female," Derbyshire said of her education.[2]

It gave her the perfect skill set for the very specific task of making test equipment sing. She composed with her slide rule and book of logarithm tables, working out what frequencies and harmonics she could wrangle from the Workshop's motley set-up. She scrawled elaborate equations in brown ink in the margins of music sheets, graph paper, and random paper scraps. Some notes in her archive are nothing but columns of numbers—frequency tables, time signatures, and various number groupings—their purposes lost to time. Many of these pages she carried around in a basket.

"She had her own complete language in the way she worked," Brian Hodgson said.

Derbyshire's math-based musicianship fascinated the Workshop staff. Scattered in so many other ways, it's where Derbyshire entered her zone. She knew—*somehow*—the way to turn a bank of oscillators and miles of tape into something not just musical, but *way out and catchy*. Bringing an "analytical gift to everything," Dick Mills recalled, Derbyshire counted the number of camels' feet crossing the screen for a documentary about the Sahara to better set the music's tempo.

Derbyshire's in good company in the Music and Math club—Queen guitarist Brian May, composer Philip Glass, and singer Art Garfunkel all have math degrees. Albert Einstein said playing the violin gave him the "most joy in my life." For Gottfried Leibniz, a seventeenth-century math wiz, the connection is innate: "Music is the pleasure the human mind experiences from counting without being aware that it is counting."

But some very non-mathy phrases—"psycho sound," "blinding music crescendo," and "human triumph, stirring"—pop up in her notes amid the numbers and equations, written in tiny and not always legible handwriting. Digits swirled in her head, but in the end, she let the music's emotional impact guide her.

Derbyshire's piano lessons began at age eight. Books cost too much for her family, so radio figured big in her life. She revered Bach, but would eventually be intrigued by the experimentalist composers. She was never in awe of them, though. Karlheinz Stockhausen was visibly annoyed when she snickered during one of his concerts.

A self-described "clever girl," she studied acoustics on her own when her school wouldn't teach it. Like Oram, she saw parallels between sound and life. Discussing a former classmate's ability to easily tolerate shrill frequencies greater than 2,000 hz—*how does that even come up in conversation?*—Derbyshire chalked it up to maternal instincts: Her classmate, a recent mother, needed to withstand her newborn's cries.[3]

##

Rejected by Decca Records—we don't hire women for the recording studios, they told her—Derbyshire came to the BBC as a trainee studio manager. The BBC typically assigned employees, often against their wishes, to the weird place that made the spooky sounds. But Derbyshire made a beeline for it right after coming to the BBC. She stopped by the Workshop on days off and "gradually infiltrated" its operations. She spent an early visit correcting errors in a book of frequency tables she found on the shelf. Her actual job, assisting at a classical music program, called on her uncanny ability to "read" record grooves. She could find the exact spot where, say, the trombones or vocals, came in. "They thought it was magic."[4]

She navigated the Beeb's administrative maze to officially join the Workshop in 1962, and would remain there for twelve years.

The BBC could be "stuffy" at times, Hodgson says. One hapless staffer was sent home for his "too pointy" shoes. Hodgson himself got in trouble for once wearing a Royal Air Force cravat instead of the standard tie. "You need to first earn a reputation if you're going to be a flashy dresser," he was told. Photos confirm an impressive tidiness throughout the studio—not easy, considering the miles of tape and countless wires on hand. Men favor white shirts and ties, while the women are also smartly dressed.

So Derbyshire swept into the Workshop with a boldness that immediately charged the atmosphere at Maida Vale.

"In my first contact with Delia, she propositioned me beautifully in French, asking when we were going to sleep together," Hodgson recalls. "I said, 'I don't think my boyfriend would like that too much.' So we both immediately knew where we were. We became very close friends."

The Doctor Who Theme: How they Made it

Grainer's confidence in the Workshop is reflected in his score's lack of details, which at one point called for "swoops." Derbyshire assumed he meant sine waves, but Grainer was no techie—he just wanted something that sounded swoopy. The score also included "wind clouds," "bubbles," and "sweeps." It did come, though, with a carefully considered rhythm. Grainer expected live musicians would do the heavy work, with the Workshop adding widdly-diddly sounds for a space-age touch.

Instead, Derbyshire got to work. To build the song brick by brick, though, she first had to create the bricks themselves. "We spend quite a lot of time trying to invent new sounds that don't exist already," she said.[5]

They began with the ominous and chugging *dunga-dun-dun* bass line that gives the tune its charge.

"We did a bass twang – but that wasn't a guitar bass, that was just a steel string we struck," said Mills, who assisted. They recorded a single-string pluck and then looped the recording and played it back several times. They slowed or sped up each playback to get the notes they needed.

"Literally, we built up the orchestration with individual notes and Delia would say 'I think we need about 64 B flats and 25 D's and B's' and things like that, and we cut them all out physically," Mills said.[6] Snippets of tape—physical bits of music you could hold in your hand—began piling up in Room 12. Surprisingly, both Mills and Hodgson say that keeping track of tiny tape bits is easy; just mark the music note on each tape snippet with a wax pencil.

With their signature hyper-precision, they snipped the individual notes to the right length, assembled them in order, and then taped them together. To give the bass line sound a looser feeling, they made very short foghorn-like oscillator tones that lead into these bass notes.

For the top-line melody—the *weee-ooo!* part—turning the dial in the middle of an oscillator produced the dramatic glissando. "Each one of the swoops you hear is a carefully timed hand swoop on the oscillators," Derbyshire said.[7] It's harder than it looks, as Workshop visitors learned when trying their hand at it. But with wax markings and muscle memory, oscillator virtuoso Derbyshire could perfectly repeat musical phrases on it. White noise generators made the hissing sounds.

Once she and Mills amassed all the swoops, hisses, bass thumps, "clouds," and "wind bubbles," they had to put it all together. Eventually, they had three reels of tape, Mills said— one had the bass, another the melody, and the third had "all the bits and pieces and the white noise—the clouds going by."

After weeks of work, they were pretty much set, except for one problem: a bum note—something wasn't in sync. Confoundingly, the culprit hid somewhere in the three seemingly endless reels of tape, with no easy way to find it. The scotch tape that connected the bits of magnetic tape— "sticky joins" in tape editing parlance—eluded the naked eye while spooling through tape machines. They did have, though, a really long hallway on the ground floor—even by the standards of large London buildings—bookended by the reception desk and Warwick Avenue tube station.

They unwound the three tape reels side by side down the corridor and walked along them, closely eyeing each of the sticky joins. About thirty seconds of music, Mills estimated, equaled 700 feet of tape. "When we came to an edit join that wasn't opposite any other join, we thought, 'I bet that's the wrong note.' And it was!"

Now they just needed to do the mix. Without multitrack recorders, they put each tape reel on its own playback machine. The herding-cats job of getting three early tape machines to stay in sync required more tiny snips of tape. With all machines cued up, Derbyshire and Mills deployed the "play" buttons at once with a "ready, steady, go!" It took a few tries.

"All we did was then play those three reels of tape together and rerecorded the mix onto a single tape, which became the master."

At least, that's the closest account I can offer. Despite a Zapruder-film-level amount of scrutiny by Radiophonic fans and the Workshop itself, some details remain slippery. Even among Workshop members, accounts can differ. Was it a string or a rubber band that supplied the bass sound? Did the final mix involve three tapes or four? Sometimes a melodica is said to double the melody (but most likely not). That's understandable—it was one of countless assignments, and not even a particularly prestigious one at the time. Who remembers everything they did at work sixty years ago?

Six decades after the *Doctor Who* theme confounded millions of TV viewers, it's fitting that some mystery remains.

"In a Weird, Fluid and Uncanny Way"

They assembled the theme piece by piece, so Derbyshire and Mills couldn't truly know what they had until hearing the final mix. Derbyshire remembered "being so delighted" listening to these "short sounds on tiny bits of tape"[8]—swooping, hissing, and thumping—pouring from the speakers in Maida

Vale. They had made, and just heard, the first avant-pop electronic masterpiece.

Grainer, who barely recognized it as his composition, is still officially credited as the sole writer due to BBC policy at the time. He offered Derbyshire half of his royalties, but the BBC wouldn't allow it. Derbyshire said she instead received a free *Radio Times* magazine.

Without the sophisticated metrics we have today, no one knows exactly how many people watched the first episode, but definitely fewer than the BBC had hoped. The Kennedy assassination happened the day before, and the world attended to other matters. But those who did tune in had their homes invaded by a sound that promised something far more advanced and less hokey than the show they got. With no recognizable instruments or hint of performing musicians—how *was* it made?—this jaunty and slightly menacing tune both thrilled and confused audiences. They had no idea of the hundreds of tiny tape bits patchworked together, or the late hours of trial and error spent in Maida Vale, coaxing vintage tape machines to cooperate just enough to materialize this new, never-existed-before music.

"Nothing quite like this as a title tune has been heard before on TV," raved *The Mirror*. "It is a noise with rhythm and melody which continually pulsates in a weird, fluid and uncanny way."[9]

Electronic music's reputation got an immediate makeover. Instead of some chilly sound collage to impress a room of tweedy academics, *Doctor Who*'s theme proved that you could turn oscillators, filters, and tape into an intergalactic dance tune for everyone. Without actually sounding anything like it, the *Doctor Who* theme beats with the same energy and attitude of the day's rock 'n' roll.

Some grouse that it overshadows the rest of the Workshop's oeuvre. Derbyshire herself considered it something of an albatross, and Briscoe called it a "both a milestone and a millstone." But it's still the first thing people know about the Workshop. Orbital's Paul Hartnoll called it "the single most important piece of electronic music."[10] *BBC Music Magazine*, from the organization that initially refused to call the Workshop's output "music"— named the *Doctor Who* theme one of the twenty works of music defining the century. Calling it "a groundbreaking piece of electronic music before the age of the keyboard synthesizer,"[11] they list it alongside works by Shostakovich, Messiaen, and Penderecki. This time, the BBC even cited Derbyshire by name.

With the *Doctor Who* theme, the Workshop was no longer where they made "music that nobody likes for plays that nobody can understand," as Mills puts it.

It lives on in other ways. You can hear the high-pitched melody in Pink Floyd's "One of These Days." Muse borrowed from it for their song "Uprising," and Mannheim Steamroller covered it. But truly recreating it can't be done. They made each blip, hiss, and swoop from scratch. Pure electricity and bits of tape were the ingredients, but the manual labor— and the tiny imprecisions that come with it—make it sound human. It's like a flying saucer being operated by people while they're still reading the manual.

"One didn't know where one was going, so it was a great journey of discovery,"[12] Derbyshire said.

Ozzy and the Daleks

"I am Iron Man!" declared Ozzy Osbourne as Black Sabbath's frontman in 1970. If Iron Man sounds a lot like *Doctor Who*'s perennial archvillains, the Daleks ("Exterminate! Exterminate!"), you can thank the ring modulator.

Just as it made Ozzy sound all metallic and terrifying, the ring modulator turned the Daleks—essentially, giant salt shakers with plungers and egg whisks for arms—into the universe's most fearsome fiends. It's probably the best example of how the Workshop's sounds compensated for the show's lackluster visuals. Brian Hodgson used the effect when tasked with giving voice to the Daleks, who first appear in the series' second episode. He instructed actor Peter Hawkins to elongate his vowels for maximum effect.

Like so many other things in the Workshop arsenal, the ring modulator was initially intended for entirely different purposes. Specifically, it was designed to enable stereo broadcast of FM signals from radio waves. Stockhausen used it to haunting effect in *Gesang der Junglinge*, as did Bebe and Louis Barron for *Forbidden Planet*'s "electronic tonalities" (like the Workshop, their work was also denied the recognition of "music"). The Daleks, though, remain the ring modulator's most iconic showcase.

5

Fragile Ribbons of Iron: A Chapter about Tape

In photos of the Workshop, tape is everywhere. Loops of it blossom from studio walls. Hyper-focused Workshop staff hover over cutting blocks during splicing sessions, or gingerly thread it through playback machines. Even more than oscillators and other electronic equipment, tape gave life to the Workshop. Loops, changing speed, and echoes were all possible, thanks to tape. It also allowed the Workshop to capture any sound to use as raw material for their compositions.

The early Workshop relied on recording tape more than anything else, so it's worth a closer look at how this technology led to a new and seemingly infinite palette of sounds, and what made it such an effective but fleeting way to make music.

First, though, how did we get recording tape in the first place?

Fancy Smokes, Water Fowl, and Nazis

Germany's smokers of the 1920s had a dilemma. They liked the stylish bronze tip of their cigarettes, but not the unstylish metallic residue it left on their lips. To fix this, a cigarette company hired freelance tinkerer Fritz Pfleumer, who used glue to keep the metallic particles in place. As a bonus, he magnetized the particles to allow for automated cigarette inspections.

With that problem solved, Pfleumer moved on to fixing the lousy recordings of his beloved opera. He reworked his cigarette technology to create a tape coated with magnetized particles that could record electrical audio signals. He obtained a patent in 1928 and sold the research to the German electrical company AEG.

The company's early efforts weren't great; clouds of toxic dust arose as the tape passed through the machine. A chance meeting at a duck-hunting club got things on track, when a scientist from AEG met another from Badisch Anilin-und-Soda-Fabrik (thankfully shortened to BASF) and they got to talking. The two companies ended up collaborating on the Magnetophon, the first decent tape-recording machine. The Nazis would use it to record Hitler's many speeches and play them back for broadcasts. Tape accommodated the long-winded Hitler better than phonographs, but the real story was its fidelity. These recordings sounded downright lifelike to 1940s ears. The Allies wondered how Der Fuhrer could be in so many places in so little time.

American soldiers solved that mystery near the war's end when they found Magnetophons stored at an abandoned radio station near Frankfurt. The technology amazed people with its ability to edit recordings in so many ways—sped up, slowed down, or cut into pieces and reassembled like a sonic jigsaw puzzle. Music's adventurers went nuts for it.

These fragile ribbons of ferric oxide freed mid-twentieth-century composers from the conventional physics of sound. It's one thing to devise a new instrument, but now musicians could break sounds down into atomic-sized bits and rearrange them into something that no one had ever heard before. They could explore fundamental questions about music: Do we need the performer? What is a musical instrument? And for that matter, what *is* music?

Like a Broken Record (and Why That's a Good Thing)

Desmond Briscoe recognized the possibilities early on. With tape, sound could be customized specifically to the length and mood of a program.

"Once you've got sound on tape it becomes an object," Briscoe said. "You can handle it, cut it up, stretch it, play it backwards."[1]

Or even better, loop it. Before tape, you had the closed groove, or *sillon fermé*—the "broken record" effect—that Pierre Schaeffer discovered while working with his disc-cutting lathe. With the malleability of tape, though, came new possibilities. A deceptively simple idea that can turn just about anything into music, the tape loop has had a profound effect on music. Today, we live in the Age of the Loop; repeating fragments of sound are everywhere. In the late

1950s, though, Workshop staffers had just begun discovering all that loops had to offer.

"Making the sample into a perpetually playing loop enabled experiments," Mills said—that is, they could easily play with tape speed, filter frequencies, or add reverb. Loops also made it easy to copy recorded snippets and find a new place for them, Mills said—a "precursor of the now ubiquitous 'cut and paste' technique."

Making the loop itself is easy—take any length of magnetic tape with a recording on it and join the ends together with sticky tape. Then thread it through a rigged-up tape machine so that the tape repeatedly circles around, running against the device's playback head.

The tape loop was so integral to Workshop operations that engineer Dave Young concocted a device specially for it. A spring-loaded arm affixed to a hefty metal stand allowed users to adjust the tension of the loop. "DoNotFiddleWith," scrawled on masking tape, doubled as its official name and a warning to curious visitors.

Typically, loops didn't reach beyond the studio's walls. When they did, though, being housed in a former roller rink paid off.

"It went out through the double doors and then through the next pair; just opposite the ladies' toilet and reception," Derbyshire bragged about one of her creations. "The longest corridor in London, with the longest tape loop!"[2]

Music relies on repetition—rhythms, musical phrases, choruses. That's because we like it.[i] Science is catching up

[i] Unless you're the late musicologist and famous killjoy Theodor Adorno, who decried repetition in music as "antagonistic to the ideal of individuality in a free, liberal society."

on why, with various studies about the dopamine our brains release when we hear familiar sounds. Tape loops heighten the effect, creating a kind of hyper-repetition. In fact, looped recordings turn pretty much everything into music. Diana Deutsch, a psychologist at the University of California in San Diego, discovered this by accident when a glitchy lecture recording kept repeating the words "sometimes behaves so strangely." It went from annoying, to melodious, and then downright song-like. You can hear it on YouTube—it's a total earworm.

But it has to be done with a loop: If you just say the words "sometimes behaves so strangely" over and over, the imperceptible variations of human speech kill the effect. "When the phrase is spoken repeatedly in real time, the words would change slightly on each repetition—in pitch, duration, loudness, and so on—so damaging or even destroying the illusion," Deutsch said in an email.

Which is to say—and this is pretty remarkable—that the simple act of joining two ends of a recording tape can turn the most mundane conversation into a catchy tune.

Tasked with the signature tune to "Talk Out" (*disc 1, track 25*), a 1964 "modern discussion program," Derbyshire collected utterances even more banal than "sometimes behave so strangely." Through repetition and doubling the voices, she turned them into a song. The twenty-five-second theme was never broadcast; the BBC passed on the program's pilot episode. A year later, composer Steve Reich premiered "It's Gonna Rain," an eighteen-minute composition that's understandably considered an early masterpiece of tape loops. As a showcase for the music of language, though, it's a bit of a cheat. Reich's source material is charismatic Pentecostal minister Brother Walter sermonizing on the streets of San Francisco. Even without the loop-induced repetition, Brother Walter's speech is pretty musical on its own.

The anonymous voices of "Talk Out" are, by themselves, not the sort that could hold a crowd on a city street corner. Derbyshire even included lots of "*ums*" and "*ers.*" None of it sounds like it should work, but "Talk Out" is a great and overlooked showcase for the musicality of everyday speech.

A Brief History of Slowing Down, from the Beeb to the Biebs

Tape manipulation can transform the world around us. Make a field recording of cars passing outside your office. Slow it down to half speed, or quarter speed, add some—or a lot—of reverb. Suddenly, the sounds of the morning commute become the vastness of outer space or the inner torment of a mental breakdown.

Today, it's easy to forget how amazing it is that we can slow down sound. We're literally manipulating time. Sure, we can speed up sound—also impressive—but sped-up sound has much less gravitas (early experimentalists played with it, and then left it to Alvin and the Chipmunks). Slowing things down makes us reconsider what we thought we knew. In 2010, producer Nikki Kaelar uploaded a version of Justin Bieber's "U Smile" that she slowed down by 800 percent, transforming the chirpy bubblegum tune into something described as "hauntingly beautiful,"[3] and a "glacial epic."[4] Many compared it to the work of Icelandic postrockers Sigur Ros.

Slowed down, we hear the world anew. Record yourself chomping an apple, slow it down enough, and you hear the harrowing tale of fibers being violently ripped from their fruit, one by one.

Mills would record the squelchy noises he made with his greased-up hands. Slowed down a little, the tape produced a comical sound. Slowed down a lot, and it was terrifying. You want a dinosaur fight? That's easy. "You get a recording of two small puppy dogs fighting and growling at each other and slow that down," he said. "And then you've got your dinosaurs."

Hodgson harnessed the power of slow when creating the sound of the *Doctor Who* TARDIS (*track 21, disc 1*), the unreliable but deceptively roomy Police Box that serves as the Doctor's time-traveling vehicle.

"It doesn't go up, it doesn't go down, it goes everywhere at once," Hodgson says of the Tardis. "I had to think: 'What do time machines do?' And I heard this phrase somewhere: 'The rending of the fabric of time and space.' So I wanted rending."

It all came together for him while watching *Exodus* at the Kensington Odeon theater, a few miles from Maida Vale. During intermission (he didn't have money for the concession stand), he mapped everything out.

Hodgson's go-to sound source was a broken-down piano discarded by a Sunday school class. He used it previously to imitate a ship grinding to a halt on rocks. For the TARDIS, he opened up the piano lid and scraped his mother's front-door house key along the exposed strings, focusing on the ones at the lower end.

He added echo to the recording. He sped up some sounds, but most of it was drastically slowed down. Resisting the cliché of a rising note ("that's just a rocket ship—everybody does that") he made a concoction of feedback, white noise, and chopped-up sine waves. "We still need a rising note," his producers insisted. He went back and reversed the feedback sounds to convey an ascent. The sound was officially recognized as "music" by the BBC in 1973, giving Hodgson a "composer" credit. And it's as timeless as the Doctor himself. More so, actually. Over six decades, thirteen actors have played the titular Doctor, but audiences still hear the sound of Hodgson's keys scraping the same piano strings.

Like One Dimension of Time Dragging against Another: The Physicality of Tape and the Benefits of Failing

When we talk about magnetic tape, it sounds a lot like we're talking about ourselves. Tape doesn't do well in extreme temperatures. It's temperamental. It decays over time. It gets brittle and shrinks as it ages. And eventually, it dies. And unlike the ones and zeros of digital technology, tape takes up physical space. Sharing that space in small, non-air-conditioned rooms was a part of life at the Workshop.

"The equipment would be spread around you," Hodgson said. "There'd be loads of little cup hooks on a batten around the wall, so if you made a loop, you could hang it on there."

Guitarists brag about playing until their fingers bleed, orchestra musicians kvetch about muscle aches. It's a badge of honor. Not so much in electronic music, though. Richard D. James, also known as Aphex Twin, goofs on the genre's lack of physicality by lounging on a couch while performing live. But before synthesizers, tape-based electronic music was an extremely tactile, physical endeavor.

"I developed a very bad neck and had to have injections of muscle relaxants," Hodgson says, recalling one particularly arduous assignment.

Repeatedly locating the beginning and end of particular sounds, lining them up on the slicing block, and measuring precisely where to cut requires serious endurance. Not to mention "a steady hand, and no sneezing," Mills points out.

Over Zoom, contemporary tape composer and Workshop superfan Robin the Fog holds up his finger to the screen to show me his latest razor-related injury. Tape music is dangerous!

Tape rarely does what Robin sets out to do with it. A digitally made loop on a computer is "literally the same zeroes and ones every single time." Tape loops, though, offer subtle changes with each repetition. These changes often improve on his original idea. The unpredictability is like an invisible collaborator, Robin says.

And like us, tape machines are fallible. They can start in perfect sync, playing tapes back at equal speed, only to gradually change speeds—sometimes too much, other times just enough to make things really interesting. This put the Workshop's engineers at the mercy of tape's whims, but it also led to flanging, phasing, and other great effects.

Today's digital technology doesn't fail. Tape failed a lot—that's a good thing. Screw-ups are where we find the heart of tape-based music. The *Doctor Who* theme worked so well, Derbyshire said, "because of the way it's never quite in sync."

"It's almost as though there's one dimension of time dragging against another,"[5] she said.

Imperfections in any kind of art—music, stained glass, custom-made cabinetry—are like a stamp of certification that a human has spent valuable time on this thing for another human to enjoy. If art is about making a connection, those nicks, dents, off-notes and time slips are the glue.

Those imperfections keep contemporary composer William Basinski working with tape.

"It's such a tactical medium—you use your hands, and the machines all sound different, and they do different things, and they play at different speeds," he said.

Tape's ability to fail gave Basinski his masterpiece, and possibly his career. He was scheduled for a job interview with an arts organization at the World Trade Center on September 11, 2001. Instead, he spent the day digitizing old tape loops while watching the devastation from the roof of his apartment building.

While filming the Twin Towers' destruction, he noticed the audio from his tape loops slowly disintegrating. With each cycle through the tape machine, more iron particles shed from the twenty-year-old tapes. The result suggests an orchestra in the distance, stuck forever in a moment, slowly fading away amid odd pops and crunches. After years of failing to interest anyone in his loop compositions, Basinski released *The Disintegration Loops*, nearly five hours in all, in 2002 and 2003. Pitchfork gave it a rare perfect "10" in 2012 and called it a "classic of ambient music."[6]

Basinski, who made a remix of the Workshop's "Time Beat" in 2021, uses some digital technology these days. But tape has a quality he can't get anywhere else. Machines and tape do pretty much whatever they want, so relinquishing some control is part of the process.

"It can do interesting things," he said. "And I always loved having some element of chance come into my pieces."

Robin thinks he and Basinski are among the last practitioners of this art form. Tape is pretty easy to get on eBay; much of it is used but you can record over it. Finding a working reel-to-reel tape machine, though, is tricky and expensive. So is maintaining them. Robin has already lost one repairman to retirement. If his current one quits, "I'm up shit's creek without a paddle."

"Without getting all philosophical about it, nothing is ever guaranteed."

Echo, "a Kind of Disembodied Voice"

The repeating audio signal in a tape echo machine, Daphne Oram wrote, can evoke a haunting memory.

She's right—echo brings a lot to the table. Prehistoric shamans sought out caves that produced the best echoes to commune with animal spirits. Early humans considered echoes "the sounds or even voices of spirits from a world beyond the cave wall."[7]

All of which is to say, echo and reverb make for some pretty powerful stuff. And they're among the defining sounds of the early years of the Workshop.

We often use "reverb" and "echo" interchangeably, but there's a difference. Echo is when a sound repeats: "Hello! … hello! … hello!" In the real world, it almost always happens outside, where sound has room to travel. Reverb is echo's indoor counterpart, where space only allows for lots of little echoes, resulting in a continuous ring until it fades ("hellooooo"). And by "artificial" we mean any reverb or echo that doesn't happen naturally—or isn't echo or reverb at all, but an electromechanical simulation of it.

For most of history, echo hunters were at the mercy of geography. To get echo, they had to go where it was—caves, large buildings, the mountains. Composers would tailor their music to the acoustical properties of churches and other spaces. The long reverberation times (often up to ten seconds) of some cathedrals led to the development of Gregorian chant (sing too fast, and all those notes jumble together).

But in the postwar years, engineers harnessed the oldest sound effect in music, saving everyone a trip to the caves. Now studio engineers could mimic the sound of a bar room or a cathedral. This allowed the Workshop—still battling notions about the supposed lifelessness of electronic music— to create the illusion that their sine waves were bouncing off physical space. The Workshop arrived at a particularly heady era of artificial reverb. Just around this time, Berry Gordy developed Motown's iconic reverb by creating an echo chamber in the attic of the Hitsville studio in Detroit. Devices like the Copicat and the Echoplex began hitting the market.

Over the Workshop's four decades, echo was a constant in one form or another. Maida Vale's expanse was put to good use, with microphones strategically placed in the basement's "echo room." The Workshop also had an early model of the EMT plate reverb, a monster of a metal sheet—about 8 feet high and 400 pounds—that sound traveled through. Knock on the door of a van and you get the idea of how it worked. A damper controlled the length of the reverberation.

Tape delay, though, proved an especially expressive tool. Here, the recording machine's tape heads are strategically placed to allow one head to play back a sound just milliseconds after it was picked up by the recording head— the distance between the heads determined the length of the delay. Remarkably versatile, tape-based echo and reverb gave bounce and energy to Sam Phillips' early rock-and-roll experiments in Memphis, Tenn., as well as a sense of ghostly alienation to the Workshop's early radio drama productions.

At first, artificial reverb was mainly used to make recorded performances sound like they happened in the real world. The real world, of course, didn't always concern the Workshop. As Oram pointed out, when you're the creator of the echo, you're no longer bound to the laws of physics. You can make the echo louder than the original sound, for instance, or last longer than any real echo would. Treating echo more like an aural abstract art, the Workshop could produce a form of reverberation that no building interior would produce, unless maybe M. C. Escher designed it. The Workshop's early work was more likely to sound like something rattling about mental corridors than something inside a concert hall.

Desmond Briscoe skillfully used artificial echo to disorient and menace audiences. His "Full Circle—The Stick Up" (*track 12, disc 1*) evokes a foggy city streetscape. Repeated "pings" likely come from wood blocks or a hammer on metal, but heavy effects keep you from knowing for sure. They appear through layers of echo, then fade away, only for them to show up around another corner and repeat again.

Accidents at the Workshop led to good things. A careless manager fails to turn down a tape machine's fader, and dreadful shrieks fill the studio. But if you control that feedback, Mills said, "you got peculiar echo effects that created a kind of disembodied voice."[8]

6

Around the Office

Chitchat around the Workshop, when not about music, tended toward certain themes.

"Nobody had a lot of money, so everybody was trading notes on how to get their boiler fixed or how to put up some cupboards," said Paddy Kingsland, who was with the Workshop from 1970 to 1981. That, and the latest "scandal about what may be going on elsewhere in the BBC." In Daphne Oram's archive, letters between her and a work buddy snarked on Desmond Briscoe. At Maida Vale, one secretary deployed the code phrase "black tulips" to warn others that the boss was looking for them. Money, DIY home projects, and gossip all fueled breakroom conversation. In other words, if you've ever had a job, this probably sounds familiar.

The 107 tracks of *Retrospective*, from start to end, tell the story of a workplace. The Workshop staff made haunting, otherworldly music, but it did so in the very earthbound setting of interdepartmental memos, budget disputes, and middle managers. Cliques formed, employees came and went, personal slights grew into long-simmering grudges.

Episodes of *Behind the Music*—bursting with onstage fistfights, debauchery, and excess—fascinate us. But do we relate to them? Michael Azerrad's book *Our Band Could Be Your Life* is a classic dissection of 1980s indie rock. That said, none of the bands in it could be my life. But the Workshop's a different matter. This humdrum, workaday backdrop plays up the superhero angle of the Workshop story. Operating under the cloak of BBC-imposed anonymity, a salaried group of employees clad in business-casual attire changed the course of twentieth-century music.

Any music analysis is something of an autopsy. We pick apart the work, inspect its various components—historical context, technology, and so on—that gave rise to such a thing. What were their work habits? The personal dynamics? What ratio of camaraderie to dysfunction sparks the perfect creative tension? The Workshop's office culture—remarkable for its ordinariness—merits dissection.

How Things Worked

The Workshop didn't come together in the manner of typical music bios—schoolmates from the same block, perhaps, or through Xeroxed ads stapled to telephone poles. Its members convened through mutual employment in a large, state-funded corporation. The various avenues toward Workshop membership typically began with employment somewhere else at the BBC, and then involved a weeklong audition to essentially see how a candidate fit in with the rest of the crew.

"If Desmond liked you, and the rest of them liked you, you might be invited back for another three months," said composer Roger Limb. "And if somebody left, then there would be the usual interviews and everything like that. But Desmond made sure that he got the people that he wanted to work at the Workshop."

At any time, the number of personnel hovered around twelve. This included composers and engineers, with the duties of each—making music, maintaining equipment, technological innovation—overlapping considerably. There were two secretaries, the director of the Workshop and the deputy, known as the Organizer.

Unlike the traditional office, the Workshop was open twenty-four hours. That allowed composers to come and go as they pleased.

"Desmond certainly appreciated that creativity couldn't be switched on between nine and five. He respected that," Mills said. "It's only in later years that we came to realize that we owed him a lot for letting us experiment—and often fail."

Composer Elizabeth Parker particularly enjoyed morning coffee with engineers, actors, and anyone else milling around. The composers usually worked alone and didn't fraternize much, she said, or share their works in progress with each other.

"Funny enough, everybody was very kind of conspiratorial about their projects," she said. "People didn't often say, 'Come and listen to this.'"

They did meet up for lunch, though. "The cafeteria was amazing!" Parker said. "You'd be going to eat and you'd be standing next to Jon Bon Jovi or Roger Daltrey or Bill Nye. You'd see all these people and everybody would just be eating their bangers and mash or whatever, no one batting an eyelash."

Briscoe rarely joined the others for lunch, Limb said, preferring to dine in his office.

"I thought that was rather strange. He was a little bit eccentric, but not in a bad way."

Offsetting the Blokeyness: Women at the Workshop

For an organization that began in the 1950s, women played an unusually prominent role in the Workshop. Daphne Oram co-founded the Workshop, and Delia Derbyshire is its most famous member. With producer Verity Lambert, it was even a woman who assigned *Doctor Who* to the Workshop. Other female composers at the Workshop included Parker, Maddalena Fagandini, Glynis Jones, and Jenyth Worsley. And in contrast to, say, Decca Records, which flat-out told Derbyshire that they "don't hire women," the Workshop even assigned women to influential positions. So the Workshop was a pretty good place for women, right?

"I would have done anything to have another woman there, to be honest," said Parker, who arrived shortly after Derbyshire left. "There was nobody else while I was there, no other women. That's a great shame, because it would have made it a better place."

Parker said she didn't experience egregious instances of bias, but noted that the BBC at the time was a "very middle-aged men kind of thing." For his part, Hodgson said he actively sought out female candidates to offset "the blokeyness" of the department, but women applicants were scarce.[1]

BBC policies accentuated the sexism of the era. The anonymity of the Workshop's members led news reports to often refer to composers as men. BBC policy also meant that composition credit for the *Doctor Who* theme—by far, the Workshop's best-known work—went solely to Ron Grainer. Anonymity also obscured Fagandini's contribution to "Time Beat," the Workshop's first commercially released pop single. Not only did she lose credit to a man, George Martin, but also to a fictional character, the presumably male computer, "Ray Cathode."

Derbyshire suggested that having women on staff expanded the range of music. In 2000, she told writer Jo Hutton that women can better pick up the nuances of what producers wanted.

"Women are good at abstract stuff, they have sensitivity and good communication," she said. "They have the intricacy for tape cutting, which is a very delicate job, you know"

On the other hand, "ask a bloke" if you want a big and dramatic sound. "Men are more into violence, action sounds, frightening sounds. I was much more into reflective sounds."[2]

Parker agreed, saying that she sometimes brought a "softer, more emotional" aspect to the music. She points to her work for the *Living Planet* nature series (*track 7 disc 2*), for which she composed more than twelve hours of music. For that, she blew on a bottle to create the sound of a tropical forest and strummed a comb to musicalize seahorses swimming underwater. Previous nature programs for the BBC featured "big, brash" pieces of orchestral music. "And my aim was to get the sound to come out of nature, so I used a lot of sample sounds."

And it wasn't just at the Workshop. Bebe Barron, Wendy Carlos, Éliane Radigue, Maryanne Amacher, and Laurie Spiegel all made invaluable contributions to electronic music. A number of factors potentially explain the high number of women in electronic music. For one, its lack of history and tradition meant less time for biases to entrench themselves. Also, not requiring access to a full orchestra allowed women to sidestep an unwelcoming system. As composer Pauline Oliveros put it in the documentary *Sisters with Transistors*, "How do you eliminate the misogyny of the classical canon?" She then points to a tape recorder.[3]

Oram wrote in a 1994 issue of *Contemporary Music Review* that technology can help women evade obstacles if they use it "as a true and practical instrument for conveying women's inner thoughts, just as the novel did nearly two centuries ago."[4]

But having numerous women in electronic music didn't increase awareness about them. Composer Suzanne Ciani remembers being asked about Oram at an event for pioneering women composers.

"And honestly, I knew nothing about her," she said. "Why didn't I know about this woman? My mentors were not musicians or composers. I didn't know women who dealt in technology, and they were everywhere. But we didn't know them. They had no visibility."

Now, though, Delia Derybshire Day is celebrated every year. And since her death in 2003, Oram has also received some of the recognition that eluded her in her lifetime. Her 1948 composition, *Still Point*, had its debut performance in 2016. She's also been recognized for her work on the Oramics Machine, a device to make sound by drawing on glass and film strips. With it, Oram may have been the first woman to develop a new electronic music system. The machine, which never went into commercial production, used optical scanning technology to translate drawn waveforms into music. It was displayed for several years at the Science Museum in London.

"Women have always been there, and we've never seen them," Ciani said. "I think what we're doing now is just uncovering some of the stuff that's there."

Who Needs Time? In Defense of Deadlines

Artistry was certainly important at the Workshop, but ultimately, everything yielded to the most unforgiving judge: the clock.

"It doesn't matter how clever you are if the goods are not delivered on time," wrote Briscoe, who died in 2006. "In these days of multi-million-dollar co-productions, there is an awful lot of responsibility hanging around your neck."[5]

Every assignment began with a time budget. Not that it guaranteed smooth sailing.

"I think my record was three days and nights without going home, and I was so exhausted," Hodgson said. Being in his early twenties, he still went out after finally finishing. "Later on at dinner, I said to my partner, 'I'm getting very cold.' So he immediately put me in a cab and took me home."

Nearly passed out, Hodgson used a hot water bottle to warm up. He still has second-degree burns from it. So what project was it that required three days and three nights of nonstop work? Hodgson doesn't remember—it was just another one of many, many assignments.

"I was doing so many, non-stop. You finish one show and you get another one."

So deadlines were a big thing at the Workshop, and apparently, they were pretty effective—by the Workshop's end, thousands of reels of tape filled its archive.

Deadlines—when they're not causing second-degree burns, that is—are a force for good. We complain, but deadlines are the backbones of our work life, and not much would ever get done without them.

The creative spark that spawned your favorite song: was it some ineffable phenomenon beyond our comprehension, or just a matter of getting to work? My money's on the latter. We romanticize the Creative Muse and repeat stories of artists' epiphanies arriving in dreams, druggy hazes, and even the throes of fever. But Drudgery—the hectoring, less fun cousin of the Creative Muse—deserves more credit. Franz Joseph Haydn was besieged by deadlines; he wrote more than 340 hours of music and invented the string quartet. Black

Sabbath had one day to record their debut album, and they invented heavy metal.

"What the unit doesn't need is a half-dozen Mozarts," Briscoe wrote.[6] That is, employees insisting on turning each assignment into timeless works of art. Things moved quickly at the Workshop. Too quickly, perhaps, to fully appreciate the artistry that went into their own work. Briscoe's admonishment overlooks the fact that even our greatest composers punched the clock.

"If you think about it, Mozart didn't, in fact, write music off the top of his head for concert performances," Hodgson said. "He wrote it because the Pope wanted another Mass for Friday. He was always writing to a deadline and a particular requirement. It's the way we were [at the Workshop], jobbing musicians or jobbing composers."

If you have too much time, Workshop composer Peter Howell said, things get overcooked. "A lot of our stuff was quite raw in a way. The ideas were very fresh, but the sound was sometimes quite raw and that in itself was interesting to people."[7]

Kingsland also welcomed deadlines. Combined with nicotine, caffeine, and a bit of booze post-lunch ("nobody drinks now when they're doing something serious, but in those days, they did"), a looming deadline brought much-needed focus. The producer gives his or her needs ("it's got to say 'science,' or it's got to say 'romance,' or whatever the program is about"), and the Workshop composer takes it from there.

"The deadline really helps because then, you know, you can more or less work out how long each stage is going to take," Kingsland said.

Kingsland knows of deadlines. His work on the *Hitchhiker's Guide to the Galaxy*, which started out as a radio serial, quickly took on a harrowing pace. Higher-ups decided to broadcast the show daily, eager to capitalize on its surprising popularity. He remembers *Hitchhiker's* mastermind Douglas Adams handing script fragments to the actors right up to the time of recording. The first two tracks on disc 2 of *Retrospective* are from the show. The first, "Brighton Pier" is airy and atmospheric, while "The Whale" is driven by a tuba-like bass line that hints at *Hitchhiker*-style quirkiness.

Freed from the Stick-Waving Conductor

Sometime around the arrival of Derbyshire, Hodgson, and Baker, the BBC quietly lifted the rule limiting employees to three months at the Workshop. It became apparent that it took some time to learn the ropes, and they were sending away some of their most promising staffers. Mills said some of the "best and wackiest" of those passing through the Workshop came from the "serious music" end of the BBC.

"Once they got to the Workshop, it was as though somebody had reached into their brain and erased all memories of five lines and four spaces," said Mills, referring to the music stave. "They just could not believe they were free of this discipline from some guy waving a stick out in the front of the band. And it was hilarious. Their leaps of imagination were wonderful."

Phil Young was among those briefly freed from the stick-waving conductor. His three tracks, each drenched in echo and peppered with metallic pings, make him one of the Workshop's unsung stars. "The Splendour That Was Rome" (*track 8, disc 1*) brings a sophisticated touch with what sounds like electronically treated timpani drums. His best is "Science and Industry" (*track 6, disc 1*), created for a 1959 science series. It's the BBC's first electronic signature tune. The first seven seconds sound like a traditional factory, with high piano notes processed through filters to sound like metal-on-metal hammering. But then you get a loping, mechanical bass that drives the tune forward, evoking the image of commuters on their way to work—maybe they're on conveyor belts, or something else futuristic. Electronic squeals reminiscent of short-wave radio briefly punctuate the pattern, which then gives way to optimistic-sounding atmospheric tones. Then the bass comes back, but now more urgent: "Break's over—back to work!" it seems to say.

So, yes, a lot happens in its twenty-nine seconds: We're moving into the future and progress is great, but—as the steady rhythms indicate—the fundamental nature of work continues unabated. As this track shows, Young made the most of his short time at the Workshop.

7

The Art of Making Something from Nothing

What the History of Electronic Music Owes to Thriftiness

Two decades before Dave Young joined the Workshop, Nazi planes shot down his Lancaster bomber over Hamburg. He spent much of the Second World War in a prisoner-of-war camp. Young made the best of his time as a POW, and stories of his craftiness are legion. He turned a military-issued tin of toothpaste into a thermometer. With his engineering know-how, he secretly built radio receivers so that his fellow prisoners could tune in to BBC news broadcasts. Other than a valve he received from "a friendly German," he did so with the meagerest of means: foil cigarette wrappings, wire, the lead of a pencil, some paper. Young and his fellow prisoners hid the radios in various places—inside a gramophone or an accordion. He camouflaged one of his radio receivers as a model airplane displayed from the ceiling. The plane's engines were actually capacitors.

Back home after the war, he turned what others called junk into useful things. He wasted nothing. When his car died, it became a storeroom for his garden. So the Workshop, which placed a premium on such resourcefulness, gladly took him on as an engineer. Even in a studio teeming with musical MacGyvers, Young stood out for his innovative spirit. Among many other contraptions, he created the "Crystal Palace," named for the massive glass structure that once stood in London's Hyde Park—an exemplar of Victorian technology. The Crystal Palace, which graces the cover of *Retrospective*, prearranges and plays back patterns of notes. Described as one of the earliest music sequencers, the device made audio montages from sounds that faded into other sounds. He Frankensteined it together with a dictation machine motor, the nib of a fountain pen, and various electronics that Young collected from the second-hand stores on nearby Portobello Road.

Hodgson used it to explore "changing aural textures" in several of his works. The device's clear plastic housing—probably just something they had around the studio—serves as a perfect display case for the Workshop's thrifty ingenuity. The Workshop was of its time and place, though, and its don't-waste-anything ethos grew out of a larger culture.

"Better Pot-Luck with Chuchill Today than Humble Pie with Hitler Tomorrow. Don't Waste Food!"

So said a wartime poster urging Britons to lay off on meat, eggs, and other such luxuries. The Germans had cut off many supplies, and the economy was lousy in general. Doing without became a way of life. Lord Woolton, the nation's first Minister of Food, provided England's citizenry with a batch of recipes—"Potato Piglets," "Chocolate and Carrot Pudding" among them—emphasizing the most available ingredients. His namesake dish, Woolton Pie, features a vegetable filling and potato crust. Spokescharacters like "Doctor Carrot" and "Potato Pete" helped with promotion. (National Loaf, once derided as a mushy stand-in for flour-heavy white bread, made an unlikely comeback during the Covid pandemic.)

Scrimping went well beyond food. To promote its own products, Britain placed heavy restrictions on importing much-coveted American guitars. "The music profession is among the first to feel the impact of the Conservative Government's economy drive," *Melody Maker* reported in 1951.[1]

In any case, few people had the money to buy sleek Gibsons and Fenders. Some creativity was required. Future session player Mo Foster needed a prohibitively pricey bass guitar for his struggling band. He made a pickup from two ex-military headphones that he placed into a soap dish, which he then affixed to a cheap acoustic guitar. Then, with a TV aerial cable, he connected it to an even cheaper radio. Voila! A bass guitar, sort of.

Young musicians in the United Kingdom learned to make the most out of assorted items around the house. Thriftiness begot its own musical genre, known as "skiffle." Jugs, woodblocks, and washboards could all be instruments. You had cigar-box fiddles and musical saws. Comb-and-paper kazoos served as the combo's woodwinds. The booming resonance of tea chests and wash tubs made them ideal for bass. Do you have a broom handle? How about a mop and a bucket? You're in the band! Skiffle's premier practitioner, Lonnie Donegan, launched a string of hits that began with one about smuggling pig iron. Hordes of skiffle groups, including those with future Beatles and one with a teenage Jimmy Page, cropped up practically overnight.

The Workshop aspired to evoke futurism and technology, all bright and shiny. But it's also steeped in the same British mentality that brought us skiffle, a homespun interpretation of old-timey Americana music. It's one of the many wonderfully weird things about the Workshop. You can see the Workshop/skiffle parallels in the threadbare resources of the Workshop's early days, as described by engineer Ray White: pebbles in a box, "mutilated musical instruments," an old copper water tank, bottles, bells, assorted percussion devices, various kinds of small bells, a penny whistle, a copper hot water cylinder, arcade tokens on a wire, saucepan lids, and watering cans. Throw in a jug and a washtub bass, and you've got a skiffle combo. If Karlheinz Stockhausen and Pierre Schaeffer patched up their differences and teamed up with Lonnie Donegan, you might have something close to the Workshop.

The Workshop's lack of resources brought disparate elements together in surprising ways. There's a photo of Oram playing a mijwiz while engineer Dickie Bird quizzically looks on. This wind instrument, with two cylinders held together by beeswax, is one of the oldest instruments in civilization. It originated in ancient Egypt and has provided music for everything from wedding ceremonies to bored goat herders.

Taking a rather circuitous route, it ended up among the Workshop's random noisemakers, producing tones to be stretched and treated into the sounds of giant alien insects and other scary creatures, for the entertainment of mid-century British families gathered around their kitchen radios.

"With limited technology, we had to improvise," Mills said. "This was forced on us by the lack of sophisticated equipment."

The most famous of this unsophisticated equipment is Derbyshire's "tatty green lampshade" that came with the Maida Vale decor. Derbyshire would clang the metal shade and treat its sonorous tone with phasing, distortion, reverb, and other effects. She called it her "most beautiful sound at the time."

"It was the wrong color, but it had a beautiful ringing sound to it," she said.[2] Among a very specific circle of music fans, it's as iconic of a musical instrument as Bo Diddley's rectangular guitar. The lampshade's manufacturer, Coolicon, touts the Workshop association on its website. Dick Mills has carried the lampshade on stage at various Workshop events. ("It was like the second coming!" he said of the crowd's reaction.) It's now in the collection of the Science Museum in London.

Jawbones, Bottles, and the Science of Swing

The Workshop's ingenuity is part of a long tradition in music of using whatever's on hand. Many of music's greatest innovations come down to economics. The steel drum was just an oil can turned upside down (granted, good steel drums today aren't cheap). Using turntables to create new music out of old fueled the block parties in Queens that gave rise to early hip-hop. Beatboxing—as cheap and ubiquitous as you can get—emerged when aspiring musicians couldn't afford 1980s drum machines. How did the *quijada de burro*, the jawbone of a donkey, become a staple of Argentina's *candombe* musicians? For one thing, it produces a great buzzing sound—but mainly, because donkey jawbones were available. You use what you've got. Of course, it's not the items themselves that created reggae, hip-hop, or skiffle, but the people who first picked up those items. Entertaining a crowd with a cigar box takes determination and chutzpah.

The resource-deprived Workshop also had to make do. It had plenty of bottles, and John Baker made good use of them. Whether by blowing on the top of the bottle to make a windy-flutey sound or eliciting a "bloop!" with a strike of his palm, Baker was the Workshop's glass bottle virtuoso. He showed up just as the BBC was expanding its broadcasting to more specific audiences.

"It was the time of local radio starting and all the stations wanted their own radio signature tunes—John did loads and loads of those," Hodgson said. For every station seeking its own identity, Baker needed a new sound. Curious listeners asked how they were made. An afternoon radio talk show, *Women's Hour,* invited Baker to explain.

First, he recorded water slowly pouring from a cider jug. "By taking just one of these sounds, all the notes that were wanted were made by playing the tape back at various speeds," he said. "The faster the tape goes, the higher the pitch. All the notes were measured and cut together in the right order."[3] For the rhythm track, he used a similar process, but with a recording of a cork popping from a bottle. The tracks are mixed, some echo is added, and *Women's Hour* has a jaunty new theme.

This is an astonishing amount of work for only a few seconds of music. Today, software like GarageBand and Pro Tools have made this kind of sound assemblage a snap. Back then, it could take days.

"Virtually every single note in it was a piece of tape," said Hodgson, adding that even the gaps between the notes were made with tape.

All the more remarkable, Baker's compositions swing. That's when musicians alternately stretch and contract the beat ever so slightly. Like a lot of jazz players, Dannie Richmond of Charles Mingus' band had mountains of swing. But it shows up in plenty of other places. Hip-hop producer J Dilla programmed his own distinct brand of swing into his beats. Dave Lombardo of Slayer can swing with the best of them—it roots their thrash metal to blues and gives it even more power.

"Swing" at one time was a mysterious, ineffable thing. To most of us, it still is, but Harvard physicists are on the case. They've quantified swing as a beat offset by ten to twenty milliseconds. "That's less than the time it takes for a dragonfly to flap its wings, but you can tell the difference in the music," wrote researcher Holger Hennig in *Physics Today* in 2012.[4]

These tiny offsets systematically keep the listener off-balance, without going too far. Like the Workshop's overall mission, it hits the sweet spot between the familiar and the unfamiliar. It keeps the brain engaged and working with the music. For drummers, it's a skill acquired only after years of experience. But in Baker's case, how in the world do you use tape to orchestrate deviations equal to the flaps of dragonfly wings?

"He had an absolute gift at being able to edit what we call off-the-beat," Mills said. "But who knows how you got there, with John's editing? His gift was that he was a fantastic physical editor with a razor blade."

The swing, essentially, was cut into the tape. A chain-smoking Baker worked wordlessly for hours to get it right. Tape moved through the Workshop's Philips tape machines at a pace of fifteen inches per second. So if a tune's tempo is 120 beats per minute, one beat equals seven and a half inches of tape. You add a little tape here, and subtract a little tape there, and you get swing. Easier said than done. Just like Derbyshire's mysterious ability to make oscillators sing with emotion, numbers alone can't explain the "Baker technique."

A devotee of both Bela Bartok and Oscar Peterson, Baker trained for years as a pianist. Where he developed his tape-splicing virtuosity is anyone's guess, but it was great to see him in action. "The tape is flying in all directions and there'd be a cigarette with a long ash getting longer," Hodgson said. "How he never set fire to the tape, I don't know."

The False Promise of Space-Age Gadgets

While the war meant that many at home did without the usual supplies, it also meant a massive global production of military equipment, including electronics. The postwar abundance was a bonanza for people like Workshop collaborator Peter Zinovieff, who frequently raided the Lyle Street shops in London that traded in military surplus. In New York, Raymond Scott, Robert Moog, and other fledgling electronic musicians took to the shops on Canal Street. At the Studio for Electronic Music of the West German Radio, Karlheinz Stockhausen composed his early music with equipment discarded by the U.S. military.

While the Workshop folks deftly repurposed oscillators, noise generators, valves, and filters to make a new kind of music, they had little use for early electronic devices that were actually designed for music making. They had access to gadgets like the Clavioline, the Solovox, and the Novachord—they just didn't want them. Others also spurned these electromechanical instruments. Edgard Varese compared them to the early automobiles that copied the horse and carriage. These pre-synthesizer instruments didn't challenge music conventions the way that tape did. For all their circuitry and science-touting hype, these contraptions' traditional keyboard layouts and Western tonalities tethered them to the past. The future of music belonged not to these space-age gadgets, but to bottles, lampshades, amplified egg slicers, and whatever else was around—for a while, at least.

Dave Young, the engineer behind the Crystal Palace, lived on the coast near a municipal trash landfill site. He spent much of his spare time there foraging. According to Mills, he kept twenty-five upright vacuum cleaners under the stairs of his home, and three fiberglass canoes along the stairs. One of his dressers caved in under the weight of speakers salvaged from old TVs.

Mrs. Young might have had other thoughts about her husband's collecting habits, but electronic music fans should be grateful for his contributions to the Workshop.

Along with the DoNotFiddleWith that aided tape loops, Young was also the mind behind the Keying Unit featured on the *Doctor Who* theme and many other Workshop compositions. This proto-synthesizer, which coordinated a bank of oscillators, improved on other electronic instruments of the time by allowing for nonstandard music scales.

Derbyshire said she had a particular talent for "making something from nothing."[5] You could say the same for the Workshop as a whole. England's last Minister of Food, a position no longer needed, stepped down a few months before the Workshop opened in 1958. A year later, around the time that Lonnie Donegan's skiffle hits dried up, England lifted its restrictions on American guitars. England could finally enjoy having nice things again. The Workshop, though, continued to thrive with its getting-by-with-what-you've-got mindset, using electronically treated metal pings ("The Artist Speaks" *track 7, disc 1*) and the sound of connecting and disconnecting amplifiers ("Quatermass and the Pit," *track 2, disc 1*) to evocative effect. The producers of BBC programs may have been shocked by the shabbiness of the Workshop's gear, Briscoe said, "but they liked what we were doing."[6]

8

Goons, Singing Dogs, and Chirping Percolators

How High-End Artistry and Goofball Antics Together Advanced Music

Spike Milligan was filling his socks with custard. The women behind the BBC cafeteria counter, who had just prepared said custard, watched with some confusion. Milligan ran back to his Goon Show studio. There, he and fellow Goons hurled the loaded socks as hard as they could at a slab of plywood rigged with a microphone, trying to capture the perfect *splat!* sound effect for their wildly popular radio show. No luck—back to the drawing board.

Milligan's comedy depended heavily on sound. As a radio guy, he couldn't rely on the goofy costumes and visual gags of old-time music hall comedians. He hounded BBC staff, sometimes getting into fights, in his quest for new and better sound effects—something other than door knocks and rattling gravel. He could hear inside his head the sounds he wanted. Finding a way for his audience to hear them, though, always lay just out of reach. So when the BBC began looking into radiophonics a few years into the Goons' run, Milligan saw it as a portal to a new world of sound.

His excitement wasn't reciprocated. Desmond Briscoe certainly respected the Goons' dedication to their craft. As Workshop director, though, he wrote that working with them "could be the end of civilization" for the Workshop.[1] At this point in the late 1950s, the Workshop was still very much trading in the classic musique concrète sound as imagined by Pierre Schaeffer. The Goons' *pops! zings!* and *splurches!* – electronically crafted or not—didn't fit with Briscoe's artsier ambitions.

But there's a fine line between the high-end and the goofball. When we talk about the history of electronic music, it's easy to focus on the Paris and Cologne studios and its other, loftier, origins. But slapstick comedy, commercials, and novelty songs also make up its history and should get their due. After all, most people first hear musique concrète not by way of Pierre Schaeffer, but from the likes of a singing dog. The Workshop in particular is a place where the cultural spectrum collapses. "Major Bloodnok's Stomach" (*track 4, disc 1*), made for the Goons, embodies the highbrow-lowbrow aspect of twentieth-century experimentalism (admittedly, this is a lot to place on twelve seconds of various sounds centered around a belch).

For the most part, the Workshop's evolution plays out pretty naturally over the two discs of *Retrospective*. "Major Bloodnok's Stomach," though, altogether breaks the flow. Sandwiched between the terror sounds of *Quatermass and the Pit* and the noirish "Outside" is a "mixture of burps, whoops from oscillators, water splashes, and cork-like pops."[2] One of the Workshop's most famous sound effects, it depicts the tortured digestive system of Major Bloodnok, a recurring character on *The Goon Show*.

The Goon Show was modern comedy. Milligan picked up a fierce anti-authority streak while serving in the Second World War, an experience that left him with lifelong psychological scars. It comes out in the Goons' subversive humor. Milligan and the other writers put much effort into sneaking dirty jokes and jabs at the BBC past the censors. Filled with absurdist humor, plots operated on their own weird internal logic. Some jokes deliberately went on for what seemed forever. Long before *South Park*'s Kenny, the character Bluebottle met his demise in each episode. The Goons never crossed over to American audiences the way that Monty Python did, but you can make the case that the madcap *Goon Show* made Monty Python possible. Like the Workshop, the Goons pushed the boundaries of their artform. And like the Workshop, Milligan cared a lot about sound. So it seems like it should have been a perfect partnership.

Milligan's show was riding high while the Workshop was still finding its footing. A partnership would surely have meant steady work for Briscoe and his staff—something that might appeal to his well-known pragmatism. Briscoe was a company man, yes, but he also held a strong artistic vision. Taking over the Workshop after Oram departed meant that his own composition work took a backseat to thankless managerial tasks and squaring the artistic needs of his quirky staff with those of the BBC machine.

But he could still steer the Workshop's overall aesthetic direction. And that, apparently, didn't involve applying resources and talents to create musique concrète versions of upset stomachs for *The Goon Show*.

So, for all of Briscoe's anti-Goonery, how did "Major Bloodnok's Stomach" get made at all? Briscoe went on vacation. That's when the Workshop received the request to soundtrack the entrance of Bloodnok, a military man of endless appetites. Dick Mills—who *was* a Goon fan—jumped on it. For assistance, he brought in a staffer temporarily detached from his regular job with the BBC's classical music department. They assembled a symphony of "cut-up burps, gloops, and explosions" short enough to fit the show's frenetic pace. "We just fell about laughing every time we played it,"[3] Mills said.

Some will quibble that "Major Bloodnok's Stomach' is a sound effect, not music. But it's not just a *zoink!* or a *plonk!* It's a scrupulously crafted composition. Keeping with longstanding comedy principles, Mills maximized the contrast in sound dynamics. As Edgard Varese, godfather of electronic music himself, put it: "What is music but organized noises?"

After that, the Workshop did very little work for *The Goon Show*. Briscoe made sure that Milligan & co. weren't going to turn the Workshop into "the Goon Sound-Shop." The Goon Show would last for two more years, and Milligan would later blame its demise partly on being iced out of the Workshop. Exactly what issue Briscoe had with the Goons is unclear, but we can guess. Mills thinks one reason for his former boss's Goon-phobia "was that he actually took the Radiophonic Workshop far more seriously than we gave him credit for."

Exactly how seriously to take the Workshop's mission was an ongoing question for Briscoe. Even as he sometimes dismissed the artistry of composing for TV and radio programs, Briscoe wanted the Workshop's output to evoke the music of the "serious" composers on the continent. A Goon collaboration could have been one step too far. He bristled at comparisons between the Goons and some of his early drama productions, specifically in the use of heavily treated footsteps, long a Goon specialty.

"We used them because they seemed appropriate, certainly not because the Goons used them," Briscoe said, rather defensively.[4]

Milligan's reputation as a difficult coworker probably didn't help his cause ("difficult," as in, one time, an enraged Milligan crashed through a glass door wielding a potato peeler, threatening to kill costar Peter Sellers). But it's also possible that Briscoe just didn't want the Workshop to get bogged down in goofball humor.

But the Goons had a profound effect on British culture. You can hear its humor in the early interviews with the Beatles, who grew up listening to the Goons. In a more direct effect on the Fab Four's music, George Martin used tape manipulation for certain sound effects when he produced the Goons' records in the 1950s. These experiments later informed his trippier Beatles productions. While others at EMI were wary of such studio trickery, Martin said comedy gave him the freedom to explore musique concrète and other techniques. Things tend to be less guarded on the sillier end of the artistic spectrum.

"Working with the likes of Sellers and Milligan was very useful, because, as it wasn't music, you could experiment," said Martin. "We made things out of tape loops, slowed things down, and banged on piano lids ... these were the synthesizers of the day."[5]

No Dogs Allowed

In the 1940s, amateur ornithologist Carl Weismann roamed the countryside of Denmark searching for new bird sounds to record. A pioneer in bird song recording, Weismann convinced Danish State Radio to furnish him with some decent recording equipment (not easy to come by in those days). Even the most cutting-edge technology couldn't protect Weismann from a very old problem for birders: Dogs. They chased Weismann from private property during his field recordings, leaving his day's results marred by angry barks.

Weismann took a razor to his recording tape to extricate the pesky dog barks from his captured birdsong. Loath to let pricey tape go to waste, he painstakingly spliced the pieces of tape—each containing its own *ruff!*—tweaking tape speeds to correct the pitches. Soon, he had assembled a version of "Jingle Bells" that would be commercially released and credited to "The Singing Dogs." Previously, Weismann recorded a collection of traditional Danish songs—also made from dog barks—for a children's TV program in 1949. This places him right in the thick of early tape music experiments. In fact, it was only the previous year that Schaeffer coined the term "musique concrète" for music made from recorded sounds.

The *Journal of Acoustic Ecology* refers to Weismann as "effectively the first composer of musique concrète in

Denmark." A few twentieth-century music experts I consulted were impressed by Weismann's early tape experiments. None had previously given much consideration to "The Singing Dogs," but one was later inspired to post a picture of singing dogs on his office door.

It doesn't seem that Weismann, who died in 1999, had any real musical aspirations. Birding was his thing, and he was very good at it—his recordings reside at the National Sound Archive in London. It's even possible that he was unaware of musique concrète. On the other hand, it appears that Schaeffer not only knew of The Singing Dogs, but takes a swipe at them in his "Solfege De L'objet Sonore," a sort of audio accompaniment to his 600-plus page manifesto of musique concrete. The ideas of musique concrète, Schaeffer declares, had been corrupted to the point where "a dog was very soon turned into a performing dog." In the background, a dog barks out Beethoven's "Ode to Joy."

The line between innovation and gimmick is a blurry one and likely says more about the biases of whoever's deciding. And nothing dissuades the cultural gatekeepers like a singing dog. Or commercials for that matter.

Ba-Deedle-Deedle-Beep-Bop! Ba-Deedle-Beep-Bop!

This generation-spanning earworm is brought to you by Maxwell House coffee—specifically, its famous singing percolator. Eric Siday, pioneer of the corporate sound logo, made it in 1959. Typical for sonic exploration of this period, mystery surrounds the exact nature of the sound (working in the fiercely competitive advertising world, Siday kept his methods under wraps). Most likely, it was a form of musique concrète employing wooden temple blocks as its sound source.

Siday's main competitor in electronic advertising music was Raymond Scott. Siday was a good bit more successful in converting electronic sounds to money (according to a *Time* magazine article, he made about $5,000 per second of music), but Scott was even more musically adventurous, going as far as inventing his own electronic instruments.

After leaving the BBC, Daphne Oram also created music for commercials; her clients included Anacin, Nestea, and Schweppes. She took advertising jobs to support her more "serious" work, and had none of the business gusto of Siday and Scott. But these corporate-commissioned pieces brim with the same creativity heard in her more ambitious work. Her music for Anchor Butter beats with a pulsing hum, similar to the score we hear on "Amphitryon 38," the first track on *Retrospective*.

Her niece, Carolyn Scales, said Oram very much wanted to be accepted by the classical music establishment. She had little regard for pop, Scales said, and probably didn't recognize any of the big stars rumored to have visited her oasthouse studio. But she was also gratified at the times when her work reached a wide audience.

"She was really pleased when she heard, she says, a milkman whistling that Nestea advert," Scales said.

Being a state-funded organization, the BBC doesn't allow advertising. But signature tunes, interval signals, and sound effects are the cultural cousins of commercials. That's true of both their function—they're there to call attention to something other than itself—and in the overall lack of respect they receive. For all their innovations, is any music more disparaged than those of commercials? "It sounds like a jingle" is rarely meant as a compliment. Not only have electronic music histories long neglected this music, even the advertising industry—hardly averse to self-mythology—ignores the adventurousness of its own composers.

Raymond Scott's former collaborator, Thomas Rhea, has complained that the "academic canon" has passed over advertising music entirely. "I appreciate everything Cage did, and Stockhausen," said Rhea, who taught music at Berklee College. "But there's a whole tradition here that's being ignored."[6]

But that's a good thing. In so many cases, "tradition" is nothing more than the friendly face of prejudice and narrow-mindedness. A discipline unconcerned with its own history, on the other hand, remains forever uncharted. Its practitioners can forge paths in any direction. George Martin leveraged his supervisors' disregard for comedy—"as it wasn't music, you could experiment"—to try new things. Likewise, many commercial composers found the indifference of their industry liberating. Rejection from a club means you don't have to follow its rules.

And Now Back to the Goons

With any functional art, time loosens the bond between the art and whatever its function was. Advertisements for the cabaret shows of nineteenth-century Paris, once taken for granted, now hang in museums and fetch a quarter-million dollars. Decades after the Goons used Mills' composition to announce the arrival of the dyspeptic Bloodnok, the artsy dream pop band Broadcast sampled the track for its "Creation Day the Travel Flute Way."

Like Weismann and his Singing Dogs, the Goons used musique concrète very early in its history. Goon Show writer and performer Harry Secombe's description of their process sounds a lot like Schaeffer's early turntable experiments: "There were, I think, four turntables on the go simultaneously, with different sounds being played on each—chickens clucking, Big Ben striking, donkeys braying, massive explosions, ships' sirens—all happening at once."[7]

The program began its nine-year run in 1951, just as musique concrète began to make waves through Europe. As with the experimentalist composers, the availability of magnetic tape supercharged the work of Milligan and company.

For all his talk of having to fight off Milligan, Briscoe praised the Goons for helping move sound "forward from the past toward something new." That doesn't mean he was particularly pleased about "Major Bloodnok's Stomach."

"Desmond returned at the end of his vacation to be met by two smirking individuals who cheerfully confessed to accommodating *The Goon Show* in his absence," said Mills, who at eighty-seven, is ever-cheerful and full of quips. It's easy to picture the fun he had putting it together. "To this day, I'm not sure if Desmond ever quite forgave us."

9

The World as Their Instrument

How the War, and then the Workshop, Altered the Sound of Life

When, in due course, man invented words and music, he altered the soundscape, and the soundscape altered man.
—Buckminster Fuller.

At about 7 pm on November 14, 1940—as families were finishing dinner, or folks were at the local cinema—bombs began raining down on the industrial city of Coventry. By the time it ended the following day, the Luftwaffe had dropped 500 tons of explosives, including thousands of incendiary bombs that burned through the city like paper. That Nazi air raid killed more than 500 people, destroyed more than 4,300 homes, and damaged three-fourths of the city's factories. It was the worst in a series of air raids to hit the city known for making bicycles, airplane parts, and cars. "Coventration" came to mean any similar act of brutality.

Ear-piercing, electrically powered air raid sirens announced each of these raids, mounted atop tall buildings, telegraph poles, and the city's other highest points. Their howls enveloped the city and summoned Coventry residents to nearby air raid shelters. Delia Derbyshire lived there, between the ages of three and five. The sirens' electromechanical wailing—the tones slowly ascending, and then descending—had a profound effect on her.

"My love for abstract music came from the air raid sirens," she would say years later. The long steady wail that gave citizens the all-clear also stayed with her. "That was electronic music."[1]

Like so much else in the Second World War, sound was an extreme experience that left an indelible mark on those who lived through it. The enormous buzz and chug of Spitfires in the air, the sounds of falling bombs, and of fire trucks racing through the streets, all remained lodged in their memories. The first wave of Workshop employees had taken it all in. They would later draw from these memories to create something never heard before. The sounds they produced at the Workshop would in turn become part of the modern soundscape.

Derbyshire, who would darkly quip that she was Coventry-born, -bred, and -Blitzed, carried those siren sounds with her after the war. She also carried with her the sounds of clogs on cobblestones. She heard them every morning as millworkers passed by her home in Preston, where her family had moved to escape the Blitz.

Much of the early electronic sound experiments resulted from their makers exorcising wartime demons. Karlheinz

Stockhausen, whose mother was killed by Nazis, wanted to create music as different as he could imagine from the 4/4 marching music he heard on the radio celebrating German soldiers. Spike Milligan's friends believed that *The Goon Show*'s violent sound effects were his way of reducing the explosions that left him shell-shocked as a soldier into something comical. Iannis Xenakis, half his face shattered by tank shrapnel, drew musical inspiration from anti-war demonstrations. His compositions reflected the chanted slogans of "great power and beauty" that gradually would slip out of rhythm and devolve into chaos amid gunshots and the whistle of bullets, followed by a "detonating calm, full of despair, dust and death."[2]

Waiting it out inside an air raid shelter involves an intense focus on sound; those inside have no visual clues about the action outside. This meant listening not just for sirens, but the whistling sounds of falling bombs (a high-pitched form of psychological terror designed by the Nazis) and the distinct sound of German planes.

"Looking back with the benefit of hindsight of a sound designer, I should have realized how the German bombers cast fear ahead of their arrival by desynchronizing their engine revolutions to produce a steady, ominous beat," said Dick Mills, who also remembers collecting still-hot bits of shrapnel with other boys in his neighborhood.

Brian Hodgson noted that he and John Baker also grew up in heavily bombed cities, Liverpool and London, respectively. "So we were all accustomed at an early age to weird sonic episodes in our lives, the sound of bombs falling, nearby explosions, and air raid sirens."

##

Long before sirens, church bells ruled the soundscapes of England's towns and cities. Starting in the Middle Ages, bells told you when someone got married, was born, or died. They warned of attacks, floods, and fires. Villagers could keep track of time by the bells' peals. Bells literally defined a community. "Cockney" Londoners are those born within earshot of the bells of the church of St. Mary-le-Bow. Bombings silenced the great bell at Bow, once called "the very soul of London," along with those of many other churches in England. It would be years—decades in some cases—before they rang again.

Church bells, which once symbolized the voice of God, gave way to the civil defense sirens operated by a secular government. Neither were originally created for music, but just as composers like Mahler and Mussorgsky found a use for church bells, sirens found their way into the music of Edgard Varese and George Antheil.

The sound of sirens—a near-daily experience at the height of the Blitz—was generated by a pair of rotors flanking an electric motor. Today, England's air raid sirens are sonic shorthand for the Second World War. We hear them in war movies, even when they're set in countries that used different sirens. Unlike bells, air raid sirens were mostly unscathed by the war. In the new era of the Cold War, they continued to stand lookout in case they were needed to shepherd residents off to one of many fallout shelters.

The first few dozen tracks on *Retrospective* subtly suggest a world shifting from bell to siren. Or, as Futurist artist Luigi Russolo wrote, when "the invention of the machine" changed how the world sounded. Physical objects resonate on these tracks. What they are exactly is just beyond the ear's recognition, though, thanks to electronic treatments. Derbyshire's favorite sound trick, the ringing metal of a clanged lampshade, recalls the peal of a bell. Her electronic manipulation of the tone pulls it into the era of the siren.

On *Retrospective,* the processed metallic *pings* that run through "Time on Our Hands" (*track 16, disc 1*)—her one TV assignment before *Doctor Who*—suggest the use of the lampshade. Shimmering tones loom for the first half of the compact two-minute track before a series of percussive chimes, mixed with the hiss of white noise, ring out a disquieting melody that repeats until faded. She made it for a documentary about the future of automation, but it's effective all on its own.

The Sound Design of Actual Life

Sometimes, Dick Mills would surprise his wife by identifying sounds outside their house with impressive precision:

> I'd say, "Oh, that's the gate on the garden of the house, three houses up." She'd say, "How do you know that?" And I'd say "I analyze sounds and, obviously, catalog them in my mind." You can't help doing it. I don't have to switch anything on and say, "Now, I must get all the frequencies down"—you just recognize it.

Spending all day deconstructing one sound after another heightens your aural perception. From waves crashing to the squeaky serenade of a neighbor's gate, the orchestra of everyday noises constantly performs in your brain. It hones the instincts for creating the sound of a giant alien moth's wings (pro tip from Mills: start with flipping a book's pages near a microphone).

For Workshop composer Elizabeth Parker, the early morning delivery of milk bottles as they clanked against metal trays outside her family's home rank high among her formative sounds. She said it's the "angles of a sound" that make it interesting. So drawn to intriguing sonorities, Parker occasionally found herself risking injury.

"Our house was scaffolded before it was quite fully built, and at night the wind caught the tarpaulins and the scaffolding creaked and groaned," she said. "I leaned out of the upstairs window to record the sounds. Slowed down, the creaks and groans were amazing!"

Renovation is considered a nuisance at most workplaces, but not at the Workshop. Hodgson and his coworkers recorded the construction sounds down the hall at Maida Vale and added them to their sample library.

"You just use everything you've got as a studio manager," he said. "If you're walking through grass, or hit something, and it makes an interesting noise, you say 'Oh! I'll put that in the back of my head, see if I can use it.'"

Whether soundtracking talk shows or a machine ripping through the fabric of time, the Workshop brought a composer's rigor to the craft of sound design—and this was long before anyone actually talked about "sound design." Now, of course, sound design is everywhere.

"We want it to sound organic, yet futuristic."[3] This sounds like something overheard at the Workshop in the early 1960s. Rather, it's General Motors sound engineer Jigar Kapadia talking to *Time* Magazine in 2021 about Nissan's electric car, the LEAF. A running LEAF emits tones sampled from guitar, piano, and didgeridoo. Besides filling the eerie silence of electric vehicles, it provides a sonic identity for the car and alerts pedestrians to the vehicle's presence. The two-second loop increases in speed and pitch as the car accelerates, delivering a sound halfway between a normal motor and something vaguely musical.

Likewise, the Workshop often turned footsteps, ticking clocks, and other background noises into music for BBC productions. There's a difference, of course, between stories and real life. It's getting increasingly blurry, though. In 2021, BMW commissioned film composer Hans Zimmer to design "emotionally engaging" sounds for its electric cars. "We have the opportunity to change the sonic landscape of this whole planet," Zimmer said.[4] All of this brings us very close to John Cage's 1937 call to corral the world's noises into a single piece of music.

The composer Matthew Herbert also anticipates a global choir of cars. He's the director of the BBC-sanctioned version of the revived Radiophonic Workshop. This new version of the Workshop, established in 2012, works in a distinctly theoretical capacity. Essentially, it's a group of folks who think a lot about the role of sound in the twenty-first century. They're excited about what electric cars mean for soundscapes in the near future. "The collective idea was that they should all be in the key of G or something, so that traffic starts to be harmonic," he said.[i]

By the early 1960s, long before Gary Numan declared that we'd be living like cars, the motor vehicle had become central to everyday life. Derbyshire used the sounds of horns (melody) and the ignition (rhythm) to create a funky proto-techno tune out of car noises ("Know Your Car," *track 19, disc 1*). She made it in 1963 for a car maintenance program, but the fun piece never aired; the BBC feared that viewers would identify the model of the car by its sounds, offending its manufacturers.

Workshop member David Cain specialized in using sound to instill pride of place. When creating an ident tune—that is, a short sound logo—for the local radio station of Sheffield, a city known for its cutlery manufacturing, he exclusively used sounds from knives (for the bass), forks (melody), and spoons (rhythm). He used only pottery to make music for the radio station of Stoke-on-Trent (*tracks 30 and 31, disc 1*), the ceramics capital of England.

His hyper-precise tape music methods work in a similar territory as John Baker's compositions. Although Cain's music was a little more mechanical, it shows a mischievous, clever mind at work. Like Derbyshire, math informed his technique, and he eventually left the Workshop to teach it.

---

[i]Like the Beach Boys, Ratt, and other legacy musical acts, the Workshop has more than one revived version. Besides the Herbert-led one, there's a Radiophonic Workshop that performs in concert. Although not officially connected to the BBC, it's made up of previous Workshop employees.

Speaking at a 2016 math teacher's conference, Cain called his time at the Workshop "seven years of heaven."

How Refrigerators Shape Our Musical Brains

While staying with his aunt and uncle in the French village of Villars, a young Edgard Varese awoke to the C-sharp note of a passing train. It made an impression; he recalled the sound as an adult when he heard a New York subway car ring out the same note. These two C-sharps, occurring decades apart, cemented the French composer's resolve to make music from the sounds around him.

The soundscape changes, and our music changes with it. As road improvements accelerated stagecoach travel in the 1700s, musicologist F. Murray Schafer said, the sound of trotting horses made its way into the music of square dancing. Schafer, who pioneered soundscape studies, also connected the paradiddle drum beats of jazz and rock to the "clickety-clack of wheels"[5] over train tracks. And the sliding notes of blues music, he said, came from steam whistle wails. How did the blues go electric? Having moved from rural Mississippi to Chicago, Muddy Water immediately saw that he needed some voltage to compete with city sounds. He ditched his acoustic guitar and plugged in.

When the world turned electric, the collective song of our devices wended its way into our brains. Schafer would instruct his students to sing their tone of "prime unity"—that is, the sound that "seems to arise naturally from the center of their being." His North American students usually sang

B natural, while his European students sang out a G-sharp. That, Schafer reasoned, is because in North America, toasters, fluorescent lights, and everything else electrically powered hums at 120 Hertz—between a B and a B flat. In Europe, those same devices sing between G sharp and A flat. Schafer called his students' instinctive reaction the "memory traces of the electrical frequencies of two continents."[6] As the Velvet Underground's John Cale noted, the hum of a refrigerator was "the drone of western civilization."[7]

Musicians, like the rest of us, are immersed in sounds—not all of their choosing—and jingles and sound effects can long nest in the musical part of their brains ("parts," actually—researchers have located several brain regions that light up to music, and continue to look for more). And then there are the sounds that force themselves into the nonmusical parts of the brain. Researchers at the University of Geneva found that sirens and similarly harsh tones engage regions of the brain that typically don't process sound, particularly areas related to pain. "We now understand at last why the brain can't ignore these sounds," said Luc Arnal, the study's lead author.[8]

Beleaguered by drug busts, Rolling Stones guitarist Keith Richards' ears were understandably attuned to the sound of police sirens. He appropriated the *ah-WOO, ah-WOO* tune of French police cars for the loping, up-and-down melody of "Street Fighting Man" (hum it, and you can hear the similarities). The urgent tone matches the subject matter of the era's increasing political street violence.

All of this may seem far afield, but it helps explain the impact of the Radiophonic Workshop. After absorbing and processing the sounds around them, the Workshop members then produced sounds that—like the hum of toasters and the clickety-clack of train wheels—burrowed their way into the minds of their audiences. The Workshop's music drew from environmental sounds, and then integrated with the environment itself. Its sounds blended with newscasters' voices and school instructional programs. UK citizens encountered this sonic stew in their daily routines, along with the whoosh of passing cars or distant conversing voices. Just as dialogue and footsteps in Beckett's *All That Fall* blended with the play's score, it was a blurry line between Workshop music and the rest of the world's sounds. (One of the earliest uses of the term "soundscape" actually comes from a 1961 essay about *All That Fall*).

One month after Derbyshire joined the Workshop in 1962, her hometown cathedral in Coventry was officially declared restored. The bells, devastated in the Blitz, now functioned. By this time, though, bells had lost much of their community sway. Sirens, meanwhile, retained their power to unsettle. Numerous survivors reported experiencing trauma when hearing these sirens, even decades after the war. But Derbyshire heard something different. Operating the Workshop equipment, some left over from the war, she summoned the ghosts of siren tones that had long resonated in her brain. Derbyshire made them new, neither bell nor siren, but something that pointed toward a new way forward, like a battered Britain carrying on into the future.

10

The Impact of the Radiophonic Workshop

"Just Part of the Fabric of Life"

In 1977, a band of teens and just-out-of-their-teens assembled on stage at the Psalter Lane College of Art in their hometown of Sheffield, England. With questionable musical skills and no setlist, they had somehow landed a supporting gig for Mancunian punk band The Drones. Now on stage, they needed to figure out exactly what they were going to *do*.

"So we thought that we can all do '*Dun-da-da-dun! Dun-da-da-dun!*'" Martyn Ware recalls, mimicking the bass line to the *Doctor Who* theme. They worked out a hasty arrangement: The guitarist took on the *wee-ooo!* melody, the singer improvised some lyrics, and the others tackled the bass and various other bits. They proceeded with gusto.

"It was bad," Ware said. The headliner's manager ambled on stage halfway through and whispered in the singer's ear: "The Drones would like to come on now—can you get off the stage, please?"

Confident that they could fend off an audience uprising, they continued on, changing the made-up lyrics to something titled "The Drones Want to Come on Now."

Ware, on the Stylophone, went on to form The Human League, and then Heaven 17 with Glenn Gregory, who played a three-string bass that night. On guitar was Richard Kirk, later of Cabaret Voltaire fame.

It's no surprise that the *Doctor Who* theme was one of the few songs these young musicians all knew and could (kind of) play. Before going on to define British synthpop, they had spent their lives immersed in BBC programming.

So how do we assess the Workshop's overall impact on music? It's worth considering. The handful of the Workshop's commercial releases—even double CDs with 107 tracks—contains only a tiny fraction of the Workshop's output. Much of the Workshop's music will never be widely heard again. A good part of the Workshop's story lies in how its output, however ephemeral, altered the trajectory of music through those who consumed BBC programming. Derbyshire herself thought about this. Discussing their legacy as they stood on the Putney Bridge over the Thames, she turned to Hodgson: "One day, someone might be interested enough to carry things forwards and create something wonderful on these foundations."

This isn't to suggest that the Workshop's worth lies only in how it inspired other, more heralded musicians who borrowed from their ideas. It's an attempt to correct the record and claim a significant part of music history for the Workshop.

By the mid-1960s, a number of musicians began exploring electronic tones and tape manipulation and were praised as pioneers for it. But the Workshop did these things long before, to a greater extent, and to a wider audience. Because of the arbitrary ways that we rank certain genres over others, though, the Workshop never received due credit in their time. TV theme tunes and their ilk—library music, commercial jingles—rarely come up when we talk about music.

Our habit of compartmentalizing things—music being one of them—makes it tricky to put the Workshop's accomplishments in context. For instance, how should we compare the Workshop's cultural sway to that of, say, the Beatles, who—by the ways we consider such things—rate pretty high on the influence scale? Both entities formed at about the same time (McCartney, Lennon, and Harrison played music together two months before the official opening of the Workshop). Both had their breakout moments in 1963 (the Beatles' first album; the *Doctor Who* theme).

The comparison gets thorny from there, though. Influence can work in very different ways. Countless musicians speak of witnessing the Beatles on Ed Sullivan and then rushing out to buy a guitar. It didn't work that way with the Workshop—for one thing, no one really knew how they were making those sounds. But tuning into the radio or TV to catch the music of the Beatles meant also hearing the signature tunes, interval signals, and incidental music that the Workshop had cooked up for the BBC. The Workshop wended its way into the culture by stealth—showing up between shows or at the beginning of the news—gradually building a secret history that runs parallel to music's flashier milestones. People vividly remember special events like seeing the Beatles on the Ed Sullivan show. The radiophonic sounds that accompanied constant BBC programming, though, slowly gathered in the collective subconscious.

Despite occupying these separate worlds of music, the two paths did cross. Paul McCartney, cavorting with the fashionable fringe at the height of his man-about-London phase, consulted with the Workshop in 1967 about tape composition. Details are vague, although Derbyshire and McCartney apparently discussed creating an electronic version of "Yesterday."

The electro-"Yesterday" never happened, but the meeting gave McCartney entry to an intriguing new world of music. He sent Derbyshire and Hodgson a copy of "Carnival of Light," the Beatles' never-released fourteen-minute avant-garde composition. They helped McCartney get it played at the *The Million Volt Light and Sound Rave*, an electronic music event at the Roundhouse in London in the winter of 1967. Few have heard "Carnival of Light," and even fewer have anything good to say about it.

The Workshop's influence is made even more clear on *Revolver*'s "Tomorrow Never Knows," a landmark in tape loop history. Here, the Beatles sneak the avant-garde into a familiar pop music structure—a very Workshop-ish combination. Still, when *Sgt. Pepper's Lonely Hearts Club Band* hit stores four months after the Roundhouse event, the Beatles flaunted their burgeoning interest in tape music by placing a photo of Karlheinz Stockhausen—not Derbyshire— in the album cover's famous collage. There's often an aspirational angle when musicians cite their influences, and in 1967, Stockhausen had more cachet than the makers of TV show soundtracks.

Beatles' producer George Martin, who honed his experimental studio chops while partnering with the Workshop on "Time Beat," also spread the word of the Workshop's ingenuity. When Jimi Hendrix engineer Eddie Kramer wanted a better guitar phasing effect, Martin suggested a look at the Workshop's archives. Kramer got results, and apparently Hendrix loved it: "That's it! That's the sound I've been hearing in my dreams!"[1]

Pink Floyd visited the studio in 1967. So did Marc Bolan, folk singer Roy Harper, Brian Jones of the Rolling Stones, and composer Luciano Berio. Hodgson said he and Derbyshire, both in their early twenties when they came to the Workshop, enjoyed the parade of notables passing through—to an extent.

"It was exciting, yeah, but we were so busy actually doing work for the BBC," he said. "We were always on the tourists' rounds. If somebody decided they would come to see us, that was one afternoon less to work on something."

Weird Sounds Made Normal: Synthpop and Beyond

Feels like a Radiophonic Workshop's
Beaming straight into my head
　　　　　—Pet Shop Boys, "Radiophonic"

During the *Unknown Pleasures* recording sessions in 1979, producer Martin Hannett placed Joy Division drummer

Stephen Morris in a recording booth. He instructed him to depress an aerosol can of tape-cleaning fluid next to the mic, in sync with the snare. Noxious chemicals gradually filled the booth, and poor Morris barely made it out alive. It all paid off, though, with the propulsive *shh-shh … shh-shh* beat that drives the track "She's Lost Control." The sound perfectly embodies the Workshop's use-what-you've-got ethos, and leaves listeners wondering what it is that they're hearing.

Hannett's lifelong Workshop fascination is all over Joy Division's debut album: atmospheric echo, mysterious blips, machine-like rhythms. He had Morris—who suffered the brunt of the producer's sonic obsessions—record each drum and cymbal separately. In 1982, Hannett made his Workshop fandom even clearer by recording 18 tracks of his own, titled *Homage to Delia Derbyshire*.

Dave Formula, keyboardist for Visage and Magazine, remembers watching sci-fi horror series *Quatermass and the Pit* when he was about eleven years old. "There were always little things popping up, new theme tunes that were obviously electronic and probably done by the Radiophonic Workshop," he said. "So my ear by this time was completely open to anything synthesized or electronic. I think it had a massive effect on me in the 50s as a kid. "

A new generation of musicians emerged in the 1990s, intrigued by the early Workshop's primitive electronics. Bands like Stereolab directly incorporated the Workshop's sounds into their music, with ethereal atmospherics and spookiness. Electronic musician Aphex Twin, who made tape loops and built his own equipment when he couldn't afford to buy it, reissued a compilation of the Workshop's music on his own Rephlex label. The Orb, Hot Chip, Four Tet, and Orbital are just a few other electronic artists who have talked up the Workshop's influence.

The Workshop's reach has been vast. You hear the sonic palette of BBC productions in the film scores of Sarah Angliss and Steven Price, both avowed Workshop obsessives. Chris Mars, one-time keyboardist for A Flock of Seagulls, told me that he became a musician because of the Workshop. Roxy Music guitarist Phil Manzanera said his band appropriated the Workshop's "very British, very Heath Robinson-style tradition of lashing bits of odd equipment together to create innovative sounds."[2] Trish Keenan, the late singer for Broadcast, recalled her thrill when her band recorded at the Maida Vale studio, "peering through the windows of locked rooms, on a hunt for the Radiophonic Workshop."[3]

But the Workshop's multigenerational influence amounts to much more than a list of musicians it inspired. The BBC's need for theme tunes and background music thwarted Daphne Oram's ambition to make the Workshop a world-class music studio like those in Paris and Cologne. At first, this clash of visions sounds like a sad what-could-have-been tale. But through ubiquitous BBC programming, those theme tunes and background sounds filled the nooks and crannies of everyday life. These weren't the sounds people heard when they attended a concert or put on their favorite record. It's what they heard while doing pretty much *everything else*— going to school, relaxing with family, driving their cars. By normalizing these sounds, the BBC gave others the raw material to take electronic music in a million new directions.

Growing up, the experimental musician Matthew Herbert's family had a radio but no TV. He never sought out the sounds of the Workshop, but they were inescapable.

"I guess you inherit that spirit of experimentation through osmosis," Herbert said, who has gone on to record albums entirely from the sounds of a pig, or a single evening in a nightclub. "I never consciously went out and bought their music or listened to it on records or tapes. But of course, it was in school, it was on the radio, it was on the TV."

The Workshop made a huge cultural impact through BBC educational programming, broadcast both in class and after school. When Roger Limb attends *Doctor Who* conventions today, he said, people ask him as much about the music of educational shows like *Look and Read* and *Information Zone* as they do about *Doctor Who*.

David Crickmore, founder of synthpop band Fiat Lux, remembers those sounds from his school days.

"We had things like *Music, Movement and Mime* where you go into the school hall and they would plug a speaker into the wall, which had a feed of what must have been [BBC] Radio 4 or whatever it was called in those days," said Crickmore, whose band had minor 1980s hits with "Secrets" and "Blue Emotion." "Somebody would narrate it on the radio and then you dance about to these weird and wonderful sounds, which quite often came from the Radiophonic Workshop."

Derbyshire had said that radio was "the most important thing in my life" growing up in Preston. Crickmore understands. He grew up consuming "vast amounts of radio" in Grimsby, England "the sort of place that you really have to mean to go there, because you wouldn't be passing through."

Many of the synthpop bands of his time also came from towns far from London—places where, for lack of anything better to do, radio and TV played an outsized role in their lives.

The Workshop provided the Human League's Martyn Ware the "kind of content that was evocative of a future that was less prosaic than the one we were growing up with in Sheffield." For most of the Workshop's existence, sounds and music were credited collectively to "The Radiophonic Workshop." That anonymity irked some of the staff, but added to Ware's fascination. "It was this mysterious kind of secret organization, almost."

The best synthpop bands came from the UK. That's not a generalization—just look at the many lists online that rank synthpop bands in history. Exceptions do appear, usually thanks to a very broad definition of "synthpop," but England invariably dominates. It's hard not to make the connection that this was a generation raised from childhood on the electronic sounds of the BBC. Many of these artists had broken from the traditional band structure—who needs a bassist? Or a drummer? Duos like Yazoo, Erasure, and the Pet Shop Boys created their own model; each had one singer while the other member took on all the instrumental music. This second half of these duos hearkens back to the one-person productions of the Workshop.

By the 1980s, electronic sounds had become so familiar in Britain that they no longer conjured thoughts of aliens or space. Bands like A Flock of Seagulls and Ultravox instead used these sounds to craft songs about relationships, passion, and heartbreak—the very human things that have made up songs since the beginning of pop.

While these British artists forged ahead in the 1980s, the biggest stars of the United States remained tethered to the traditional guitar-bass-drums model of music combos—as well as to ideas about "authenticity" and "real" musical instruments. On the occasions when synths did come to the forefront in the U.S., they were treated as a kind of nerdy novelty. Devo's jerky movements, talk of "de-evolution," and whatever those flower pot hats were all about—these all point pretty clearly to "nerdy novelty."

Germany's Kraftwerk, who inspired everything from mid-career David Bowie to hip-hop, also showed little interest in normalizing electronic sounds. Forever dedicated to their man-machine schtick, the quartet cultivated a robotic stage presence described as "post-human musical theater" and built a career on celebrating technology's wonders. Kraftwerk's breakout 1974 album, *Autobahn* presented electronic music as the sound of the future.

By that time, though, teenagers in England had grown up with the Workshop. To them, electronic sounds weren't of some post-human future, but the stuff of everyday life—local news, tea time social gatherings, and attending school. As early as 1962, the Workshop showed that it was no longer limited to laser blasts and mental breakdowns. That's when it scored the BBC's entry in the 1962 Ideal Home Exhibition (*track 15, disc 1*, by Fagandini), Britain's annual showcase of domesticity. And residents of the UK regularly awoke to tunes like the theme to *Good Morning Wales* (Baker, 1972, *track 39, disc 1*), making these sounds literally the first thing that people heard each day.

As Adrian Utley of trip-hop pioneers Portishead put it, the Workshop was just "part of the fabric of life." The Workshop aesthetic appealed to him early on. "It was dark and it was kind of bleak, even when it wasn't supposed to be."

Many of the Workshop sounds lurk hazily in Utley's memory, like something long ago that you know happened, but details have faded. He semi-remembers a show, possibly about antiques, that opened with a tune built out of old clock sounds.

"Radiophonic music was omnipresent in our everyday life, really," he said. "It was in radio adverts, TV programs, and I didn't even know what it was when I was a kid. It's just there, this strange sound, you know. I can't really quote too many specific pieces of music. I just know them in my head."

11

Team Tape versus Team Synth

One day in 1970, a new BBC official arrived at the Workshop for a routine visit—"his introductory 'I-must-see-what-my-fiefdom-encompasses' tour," said Hodgson. Seizing the opportunity, Hodgson and Derbyshire rolled out the EMS VCS3, a shiny new voltage-controlled synthesizer that they had brought to the Workshop.

Housed in a wooden case and sporting a wall full of dials, it's the snazzy 1960s technology you see in the labs of James Bond movies. To shape the sound, you plug pins into a grid resembling a Battleship game board. To demonstrate, Derbyshire knocked out an impressive medley of *whooshes* and *pings*. The BBC ordered two for the Workshop.

This moment in Workshop history signals the eventual synthesizer takeover that would transform the Workshop's operation and sound. In Workshop fandom, a growing cult since the 1990s, the switch from tape manipulation to synthesizers draws a line: you're either Team Tape or Team Synth. It's a lot like the Roth-versus-Hagar debate among Van Halen fans.

The synthesizer was a long time coming. Mark Twain lost a fortune investing in the late-nineteenth-century Telharmonium, a massive electronic instrument designed to pipe music into homes through telephone lines. In the 1950s, a half-million dollars went into building the room-sized RCA Mark II at the Columbia-Princeton Electronic Music Center. By 1970, these impractical behemoths made way for a sleek new breed of synth that included the VCS3 and the Minimoog. They promised to democratize music and—rather optimistically, it turns out—create any sound imaginable. Users would have a full orchestra—and more!—at their fingertips.

Derbyshire didn't buy it, this musical Utopianism. She helped introduce synthesizers to the Workshop, but synthesizers eventually drove her out. Derbyshire found more magic in the sounds she got from an old lampshade and recording tape than she did in all the high-tech circuitry. These new machines offered no mystery, just squeaks and buzzes. She couldn't "get inside" the sound of synthesizers the way she could with a ringing piece of metal. Derbyshire dismissed the typical synthesizer as a fad, little more than a "glorified electric organ."

"What I hate is the way it went eventually, just pressing a button to generate a sound," she told *Doctor Who Magazine*. "I don't like the idea of replacing a musician with presets."[1]

For many fans, part of the Workshop's mystique comes from how a group of clever people carved a new musical path with very little. Actually working in those conditions, though, wasn't so glamorous. Hodgson holds little nostalgia for long days of getting by with antiquated equipment. To him, synthesizers were a practical necessity that—when used right—fostered creativity. He began lobbying in the mid-1960s for an equipment upgrade, largely to no avail.

"We don't have money to buy things like synthesizers from America!" BBC execs told him. So he and Derbyshire brought in their own synth—the VCS3 that they would show off to the BBC official. They acquired it through their side gig, Unit Delta Plus, a freelance electronic music studio they formed with future synth pioneer Peter Zinovieff. Workshop members described director Desmond Briscoe as a "benevolent dictator." He kept a tight ship, but tolerated outside projects "with a nod and a wink." Ventures beyond the Workshop, he rightly figured, led to new ideas. That was certainly the case with Unit Delta Plus, as it was Zinovieff—often called "Britain's Bob Moog"—who designed the VCS3 and founded the pioneering synthesizer company Electronic Music Studios (EMS).

The Attic Tapes

On *Retrospective*, the first voltage-controlled synthesizer shows up on track 39 on the first disc, "Dance from Noah" from 1971. Derbyshire created the music for an educational program based on the Biblical story of Noah. She also cooked up another version for *EMS LP1*, a promotional record for her pal Zinovieff. The track was rediscovered in 2008, seven years after Derbyshire's death at age sixty-four. It was among the 267 tape reels found stuffed in cereal boxes in her attic. Each about thirty minutes long, some in pretty battered shape, the tape reels now reside in the Manchester

University archives. They contain everything from ambient soundscapes to "really aggressive, nasty rhythm tracks,"[2] as described by archivist David Butler.

Besides the dramatic circumstances of the "attic tapes" discovery, "Dance from Noah" in particular made a splash among British electronic music fans. Incredulous that something so modern-sounding could have been produced at that time, some folks charged that it was a hoax (even the electronic music community has its conspiracy theorists). "Dance from Noah" is, in fact, real. With a driving rhythm over a wavering, cheerful melody, commentators described it as the first techno dance track, and something that sounds like a release "coming out next week on Warp Records."[3] Both are exaggerations, but the track is a great example of how forward-sounding Derbyshire's work was.

The early synthesizers came with a steep learning curve, and played only one note at a time. It took time for the Workshop to fully switch to synths. Roger Limb did a temporary Workshop stint in 1972 while on a break from his regular BBC gig as a TV announcer. Even after the VCS3's arrival, tape-cutting still ruled the Workshop.

"What it did, it did very well, but it didn't do an enormous number of things," Limb said of the synth. "It would make some interesting sounds, but quite often I would think, 'Oh, I wish it would do this, or why can't it do that?' It was limited in its way."

When Limb returned to the Workshop two years later as a permanent staffer, though, the synths dominated. Room 10 of the studio housed the massive EMS Synthi 100, the world's largest voltage-controlled synthesizer at that point. It was nicknamed "the Delaware" for the road that ran parallel outside the studio. The Synthi 100's British origins gave it an edge over a Moog synth, which the BBC was also considering.

"There was a new generation of more reliable synthesizers arriving at that time," Limb said. "By the time '76, '77 arrived, I don't think anybody was cutting up tape anymore."

By that point, Derbyshire had had enough. Like Oram, she chafed at the musical limitations of working with the Drama department, as well as an increasingly cautious BBC "run by committees and accountants." Combined with the synthesizers, it was all too much.

"Something serious happened around '72, '73, '74," she said in 1993. "The world went out of tune with itself and the BBC went out of tune with itself."[4]

Baker, who marveled his coworkers with his tape-cutting prowess, also found synthesizers cold and unappealing. The technology had changed, as well as the whole Workshop way of working. The BBC was expanding. More assignments and shorter deadlines didn't allow the time that meticulous tape manipulation required.

There were also skills and labor to consider. Baker and Derbyshire each spent a decade at the Workshop perfecting the arcane alchemy of converting inches of tape to notes of music. Synthesizers meant starting all over again. But it's hard to think of an alternate scenario where tape music could have continued on. The entry point was always too high—too much work, skills, and time were required to make tape music the ubiquitous force that synths became.

And for both Derbyshire and Baker, problems with alcohol exacerbated workplace stresses. Derbyshire resigned in 1972, and Baker was fired in 1974.

Paddy Kingsland blamed burnout for his coworkers' problems. "I think if it all happened earlier, they'd have jumped in on the synthesizers and used them very creatively alongside tape and all that stuff."

Despite his reputation as a bureaucrat, Kingsland said, Briscoe was "very sympathetic" toward Derbyshire and Baker. "He did what he could," Kingsland said. "He really tried to help them, and gave them as much leeway as possible during those years when it was all a bit turbulent."

A Studio to Envy

Hodgson left in 1972, about the same time as Derbyshire, mainly out of a need to move on. He invited Derbyshire to go in with him on Electrophon, his new music studio. She halfheartedly worked with him on the soundtrack to the horror film *Legend of Hell House* and then left to take on various jobs, including the improbable position of radio operator for a gas line construction project.

Hodgson returned a few years later as second-in-command. He did so only on the condition that the BBC put some significant money into updating the Workshop.

"In the early days, your biggest problems were with the equipment or the technology," said Hodgson, who took over as head of the Workshop when Briscoe retired in 1984. "You couldn't really concentrate on the music or the sound, or anything. When I completely re-equipped the Radiophonic Workshop, the problems became musical ones, which is how it always should have been."

Under Hodgson's leadership, the Workshop stocked up on polyphonic synths in the 1970s, samplers in the 1980s, Apple computers in the 1990s. Once equipped with discarded junk, the Workshop now had what Yamaha's chief engineer called the most sophisticated electronic music studio in Europe.

"There were only a couple of PPG samplers—I had one, the Pet Shop Boys had the other, and then another one was in Germany," said Elizabeth Parker, whose Workshop tenure stretched from the end of the tape era and into the synth and computer years. "We had various pop people coming in and being very envious of what we actually had there. It was really impressive, actually."

At Maida Vale for their first *John Peel Sessions* performance, the Human League immediately requested a Workshop tour. "To us, it was like the sorcerer's workshop—we could only imagine," said Martyn Ware, recalling how he and his bandmates compared it to their own paltry setup. "We walk into a room with probably 40 different synthesizers, and patch bays, and all that stuff. That was an inspiring moment."

But as technology advanced, it also got more accessible, Parker said. "It started to become slightly homogenized."

"They were all pretty much the same in each studio, which meant you had to work quite hard to have a different sound from everyone else," Parker said. "I joined the Workshop to create sounds, and you could do that with tape. It was much harder to do that when you've got a synthesizer, which had pre-programmed sounds that everybody else also had."

That said, the Workshop did continue to create new sounds by programming them into the synthesizers. When they sent synthesizers out for maintenance, Hodgson said he'd get compliments about the new sounds. Rock bands, the servicemen told him, rarely strayed from the sounds of the presets.

The new batch of Workshop composers also made good use of the Vocoder, continuing the tradition of musically repurposing equipment from the Second World War. The BBC gifted it to the Workshop unprompted, possibly to preempt complaints about resources.

Developed by Bell Labs, the Vocoder encoded messages during the war by scrambling and then reassembling speech. Voices become robotic in the process. Seeing its musical potential early on, Wendy Carlos used it in her *Clockwork Orange* score. When the Workshop's Peter Howell featured it in his "Greenwich Chorus" (*track 60 disc 1*) for the program *Body in Question*, confused viewers—years before AutoTune saturated pop music—jammed the phone lines wanting to know what they just heard. Howell saw the "mind-boggling" response as evidence that nothing fascinates people like something that sounds human "but you're not quite certain if it is or not."[5]

To my ears, the synth era doesn't have the same out-of-the-blue newness as the earlier tape-and-oscillators compositions. This isn't just a case of the-old-way-is-better; there's something genuinely different about the Workshop's pre-synthesizer days. Once you get past the first few tracks, which still owe a debt to Pierre Schaeffer's influence, the Workshop's early work sounds like nothing else. The synthesizer tracks, though, prompt comparisons: 1970s prog rock, 1980s dance pop, and various American TV scores all come to mind when listening to the second disc. It's not that the Workshop was copying anyone, it's just that everyone else was using the same technology.

To be clear, though, there are some really good tracks from the later years.

"For Love or Money" (*track 53, disc 1*), for an episode of *Omnibus* about the smuggling of artifacts for the art market, blends harpsichord, and synthesizer. Composed in 1977, it has a strong ambient feel, created not long after Brian Eno's *Another Green World* pioneered the ambient genre.

"I didn't want to go all the way down the electronic path, and quite often, I would incorporate a conventional instrument inside radiophonic packaging," Limb said. "Whether we influenced [Eno] or he influenced us, I think it was a bit of a two-way thing. But certainly I had a lot of admiration for what he does and continues to do."

Richard Attree, the last composer hired by the Workshop, brought with him rock, world music, and other influences. All feature on his seven tracks on disc 2 of *Retrospective*. Impressed by his audition tape, Hodgson offered him a job. Unusual for Workshop staffers, Attree had no previous BBC experience. Adding him to the Workshop mix, Hodgson said, was like "introducing a bouncy Boxer puppy into a pack of well-trained Labradors."[6] Soon, though, the other staffers appreciated the new ideas that came with the outside hire. Attree's skittishness about leaving the feral life of a freelance electronic musician changed when he discovered what he could do with BBC resources, like working with a gospel choir ("That was incredible!") for a documentary about Martin Luther King Jr. Plus, not only could he now afford a car, the job gave him unlimited access to hardware.

"All the composers had their own studio, and you could do it however you wanted," he said. "You could have the equipment you wanted. It was a dream come true, really."

For a while at least. Synthesizers made it easier for the Workshop to produce music, but eventually, they also made it easier for everyone else. That would cause problems.

12

The End, and a New Appreciation

The annals of music legends bear no shortage of dramatic ends: plane crashes, overdoses, being secretly and slowly poisoned by a bitter and less talented rival—the list goes on. But fittingly, the Workshop met a more prosaic demise: a round of mass layoffs, or as they say in England, "redundancies."

"It had shrunk quite a lot the last year or so," Richard Attree said. "Everybody was very isolated and never saw anybody much. It was coming to an end—we could all feel that."

A new BBC manager hired from the world of retail chains showed up at the Workshop. "She said, 'Right, well, prove that you're needed.'"

So the remaining composers, including Parker, Limb, Kingsland, and Attree, put together an elaborate audiovisual presentation to demonstrate their worth. "It was this really cutting-edge piece of music. Who else could have done that at that time?"

At the presentation's end, the manager quietly jotted down equations, dividing costs by hours of labor. She displayed the results on a whiteboard. "We just knew at that point," Attree said.

She appeared again months later, accompanied by two men. "They knocked on everybody's door: 'Well, I'm very sorry to have to tell you we're making you redundant.' It was a bit of a shock. We weren't necessarily expecting it. It was a bit brutal just before Christmas."

Parker was the last composer with the Workshop when it closed for good in 1998. Track 38 on disc 2, "Assignment (Kofi Annan)" is her final project as a Workshop employee. She barely remembers making it.

The BBC considered the Workshop one of its crown jewels in the 1980s, shuttling important visitors to the studio for tours. But synthesizers had grown common by the 1990s, as did freelance musicians working for cheap. This, plus new BBC policies that pitted departments against each other for resources, rendered the in-house services of the Workshop— once the best deal at the BBC—a gratuitous expense.

"There were too many other people doing the same job as well for a quarter of the money, and we couldn't have competed with that," Parker said. "I suppose we were very fortunate because we were paid a salary. Most composers don't get a salary."

An unceremonious end for sure, but one that kicked off a newfound appreciation for the Workshop.

##

The Workshop officially closed its doors in 1998, and this thing that spanned generations was suddenly gone. Almost immediately, there emerged a newfound appreciation for it. Composer Mark Ayres, listed as *Retrospective*'s producer, was called in to sort out and archive the Workshop's many, many reels of tape. The works of individual Workshop members were compiled and commercially released. Other musicians crib from the Workshop's vast reserve of ideas and techniques—as they have since its beginning. Only now, they proudly cite the Workshop by name as an influence.

When Daphne Oram spent hours after midnight in the BBC's Broadcasting House improvising a rig of tape recorders to compose with, she did it out of necessity. There was no other good way to produce her kind of music at the time. That some four decades later, the everywhereness of electronic music would make the Workshop unnecessary just shows how successful the BBC composers were.

The BBC first broadcast these sounds in the late 1950s— very cautiously—through Oram and Briscoe's early experiments. It introduced them with lengthy explanations bordering on apologies, and audiences responded with letters of outrage at this "fearful noise." By the time it closed, the Workshop sounds blended seamlessly with the lives of the BBC's audiences. The rest of the world had caught up.

Long before electronic music figured its way into countless genres, there was a good chance that BBC audiences would hear on any given day something entirely different from what they had ever heard before. It might even be something that made them rethink what music was. They could hear a mechanized automated rhythm that would become the foundation of dance music years later. They might hear sampling long before it was called that.

The Workshop merged the ordinary and the bizarre like no one had before. It took things that typically get thrown out—busted equipment, empty bottles—and created otherworldly melodies from it. Noises snatched from the pith and marrow of real life—automobile engines, breath, construction noises—were turned into actual music. Listening to the Workshop decades after its close is a useful reminder to also listen more closely to our present-day surroundings, whether it's traffic outside, door squeaks, or the beepy tune that tells us when the oven's ready.

In recent years, we've seen reassessments of the Workshop. In some circles, Oram is now recognized as a visionary. Histories of electronic music have been updated to place the Workshop along the likes of Edgard Varese, Stockhausen, and Kraftwerk. Delia Derbyshire Day is observed every year. A street in her hometown of Coventry has been named Derbyshire Way.

On its surface, the Workshop probably didn't look much like Oram's childhood vision of the giant machine that could generate any sound she wanted. For most of its existence, the Workshop was underfunded, taken for granted, and operated by a motley assortment of characters who passed through it over the decades. But it epitomized the ideas that Oram outlined in her research paper to the BBC—one of her thwarted attempts to convince her employers to get onboard with her vision: "Rhythms become anything the composer can visualize without them having to be playable," she wrote. "Theoretically any sound, musical or otherwise, is within his grasp."

The Workshop provided sounds for everything from the day's news events to the *thwips!* and *thwaps!* of futuristic laser weaponry. It helped shape decades of popular and experimental music. Audiences were frightened, confused, and delighted. Clearly, the machine of infinite sounds that Oram imagined had been built.

Acknowledgments

A big thanks to everyone who shared their time, knowledge, and support: Brian Hodgson, Dick Mills, Elizabeth Parker, Roger Limb, Paddy Kingsland, Richard Attree, Carolyn Scales, James Bulley, Frances Morgan, Jim Irvin, Matthew Herbert, Adrian Utley, David Crickmore, Brian Kane, Jo Hutton, Tina Dockstader, Justin Brierly, Robin Scott aka M, Diana Deutsch, Marc Weidenbaum, William Basinski, Robin the Fog, Suzanne Ciani, Alex Temple, Martyn Ware, Nigel Ipinson Fleming, David Butler, Dave Formula, Chris Mars, Steve Geringer, and Tanya Allen.

Notes

Introduction: An Improbable Stew

1   Sinker, Mark. 1992. "Deep Background Noise," *Wire*, 96,
     pp. 36–7.

Chapter 1

1   The Daphne Oram Trust website, daphneoram.org.

2   BBC Radio. 2008. "Wee Have Also Sound-Houses."

3   Candlish, Nicola. 2012. "The Development of Resources for
     Electronic Music in the UK, with Particular Reference to the
     Bids to Establish a National Studio," PhD Thesis, Durham,
     England: Durham University.

4   Hutton, Jo. January 19, 2004. "Daphne Oram: Innovator, Writer
     and Composer," *Organised Sound*, 8, pp. 49–56.

5   Niebur, Louis. *Special Sound: The Creation and Legacy of
     the BBC Radiophonic Workshop* (Oxford, England: Oxford
     University Press, 2010).

6   Ibid.

7   Jennifer Iverson. *Electronic Inspirations: Technologies of the Cold War Musical Avant-Garde* (Oxford: Oxford University Press, 2018).

8   Ibid.

9   Branigan, Kevin. *Radio Beckett: Musicality in the Radio Plays of Samuel Beckett* (Bern: Peter Lang AG, 2010).

10 Morin, Emilie. January 2014. "Beckett's Speaking Machines: Sound, Radiophonics and Acousmatics," *Modernism/modernity*, 21, pp. 1–24.

11 Briscoe, Desmond, and Curtis Bramwell-Roy. *The BBC Radiophonic Workshop: The First 25 Years: The Inside Story of Providing Sound and Music for Television and Radio, 1958–1983* (London: BBC Worldwide, 1983).

12 Morin. *Modernism/modernity.*

13 BBC Radio. 2008. "Wee Have Also Sound-Houses."

14 BBC 100. "Maida Vale." https://www.bbc.com/historyofthebbc/buildings/maida-vale

15 Ray White, www.Whitefiles.org.

Chapter 2

1   Wilson, Dan. August 2011. "The Woman from New Atlantis." *Wire*, 330, pp. 28–35.

2   Bulley, James. 2016. "Progress Music": Daphne Oram, Geoffrey Jones, and "Trinidad and Tobago." Bricks from the Kiln. pp. 5–24.

3   BBC Radio. 2008. Radio documentary, "Wee Have Also Sound-Houses."

4   Ibid.

5   Millais, Malcolm. *Le Corbusier, the Dishonest Architect* (Newcastle upon Tyne, England: Cambridge Scholars Publishing, 2017).

6   Hutton, Jo. "Radiophonic Ladies." *Sonic Arts Network*. https://www.sonicartsnetwork.org/ARTICLES/ARTICLE2000JoHutton.html (February 24, 2000).

7   Briscoe and Bramwell-Roy. *The BBC Radiophonic Workshop.*

8   Daphne Oram archives Goldsmiths University of London. Part of correspondence with the BBC in regard to the history of the BBC Radiophonic Workshop.

9   Babbitt, Milton. February 1958. "Who Cares If You Listen?" *High Fidelity*, 40, pp. 38–40, 126–7.

Chapter 3

1   Niebur. *Special Sound*, p. 84.

2   BBC. "*Alchemists of Sound.*" https://www.dailymotion.com/video/x5579ti.

First broadcast October 19, 2003.

3   Martin, George. *Playback* (Guildford, England: Genesis Publications, 2002).

4   Womack, Kenneth. *The Life of Beatles Producer George Martin, The Early Years, 1926–1966* (Chicago, IL: Chicago Review Press, 2017).

5   Lewisohn, Mark. *Tune In, The Beatles All These Years* (Boston, MA: Little, Brown and Company, 2013).

6   Briscoe and Bramwell-Roy. *The BBC Radiophonic Workshop.*

7   Fish, Scott K. Modern Drummer Legends (Boca Raton, FL: Modern Drummer Media, 2020), p. 30.

8 Sherman, Bernard D. 1997."Tempos and Proportions in Brahms: Period Evidence." Early Music, 25, 3, pp. 462–477 .

9 *Daniel Gregory Mason "The Tyranny of the Bar-Line"* The New Music Review and Church Music Review (London: Novello, Ewer & Company, 1909), p. 31

10 Ignacy Jan Paderewski. "Tempo Rubato." Chapter contributed to Henry T. Finck's book *Success in Music and How It Is Won* (New York: Scribner's, 1909).

11 Irvin, Jim. *The Mojo Collection: The Greatest Albums of All Time ... and How They Happened* (New York: Canongate US, 2003).

12 Meyer, David N. *The Bee Gees: The Biography* (Boston, MA: Da Capo Press, 2013).

13 Buskin, Richard. *Classic Tracks* (London: Sample Magic, 2013).

14 Brennan, Matt. *Kick It: A Social History of the Drum Kit.* (New York: Oxford University Press, 2020).

15 Briscoe and Bramwell-Roy. *The BBC Radiophonic Workshop.*

Chapter 4

1 "Verity's Tune is Way Out—of This World!" *Daily Mirror.* December 7, 1963. https://whitefiles.org/rwz/1963_veritys_tune.pdf.

2 "Delian Mode." *Surface Magazine.* May 2000. http://delia-derbyshire.net/sites/interview_surface.php.html.

3 Hutton, Jo. *Sonic Arts Network.*

4 "Delian Mode" *Surface Magazine.*

5 BBC. *Tomorrow's World. First Broadcast 1965.* https://m.youtube.com/watch?v=qsRuhCflRyg.

6 *Masters of Sound on the Doctor Who: The Beginning Box Set DVD (clip on YouTube).* https://m.youtube.com/watch?v=xkIE kLww3lg.

7 Ibid.

8 "Soundhouse" *Doctor Who Magazine.* May 12, 1993, Issue 199, pp. 14–16.

9 "Verity's Tune Is Way Out," *Daily Mirror.* December 7, 1963.

10 Sweet, Matthew. March 16, 2002. "Queen of the Wired Frontier," *The Guardian.*

11 Parr, Freya. March 23, 2019. "1918–2018: 20 Works That Defined a Century," *BBC Music Magazine.*

12 "Soundhouse" *Doctor Who Magazine.*

Chapter 5

1 Briscoe and Bramwell-Roy. *The BBC Radiophonic Workshop.*

2 Holmes, Thom. Electronic and Experimental Music (Fourth Edition) (London: Routledge, 2012).

3 Lyons, Margaret. "The Man Who Slowed Down Justin Bieber" (*Entertainment Weekly*, August 18, 2010). https://ew.com/arti cle/2010/08/18/justin-bieber-u-smile-slow/

4 *Sigal*, Jason "Slowed-Down Bieber: A Glacial Victory for Fair Use" (*Huffington Post*, August 26, 2010). https://www.huffpost. com/entry/sloweddown-bieber-an-epic_b_695695.

5 "Soundhouse." May 12, 1993. *Doctor Who Magazine*, 199.

6 Richardson, Mark. "Disintegration Loops." *Pitchfork*, November 19, 2012. https://pitchfork.com/reviews/alb ums/17064-the-disintegration-loops/.

7 Blesser, Barry, and Salter, Linda-Ruth. *Spaces Speak, Are You Listening?* (Cambridge, MA: MIT Press, 2009).

8 Reynolds, Simon. "Sorcerers of Sound" (*The Guardian*, February 19, 2008). https://www.theguardian.com/culture/2008/sep/20/bbc.doctorwho.

Chapter 6

1 Whitefiles.com https://whitefiles.org/rwb/2/index.htm.

2 Hutton, Jo. *Sonic Arts Network*.

3 Rovner, Lisa. *Sisters with Transistors* (Metrograph Pictures, 2020).

4 Oram, Daphne. 1994. "Looking Back … To See Ahead" *Contemporary Music Review*, 11, pp. 225–8.

5 Briscoe and Bramwell-Roy. *The BBC Radiophonic Workshop*.

6 Ibid.

7 BBC Radio 3 (2004). "Free Thinking—BBC Radiophonic Workshop." https://www.bbc.co.uk/programmes/b041y0tl.

Chapter 7

1 Melody Maker, November 1951, as quoted by Tony Bacon in Reverb.com. https://reverb.com/news/the-british-guitar-embargo-when-brits-were-banned-from-buying-american.

2 Hodgson, Brian. July 6, 2001. "Delia Derbyshire" *The Guardian*.

3 Baker, John. *The John Baker Tapes* (England: Trunk Records, 2008).

4 Hennig, Holger. 2012. "Musical Rhythms: The Sciences of Being Slightly Off," *Physics Today*, 65, 7, pp. 64–5.

5 "Soundhouse." May 1993. *Doctor Who Magazine*.

6 Briscoe and Bramwell-Roy. *The BBC Radiophonic Workshop*.

Chapter 8

1 Briscoe and Bramwell-Roy. *The BBC Radiophonic Workshop*.

2 Ibid.

3 Marshall, Steve. "The Story of the BBC Radiophonic Workshop" (*Sound on Sound*, April 2008) https://www.sound onsound.com/people/story-bbc-radiophonic-workshop.

4 Briscoe and Bramwell-Roy. *The BBC Radiophonic Workshop*.

5 Southall, Brian. *Abbey Road* (London: Omnibus Press, 2010).

6 Raymond Scott website https://www.raymondscott.net/featu res/tom-rhea/

7 Ventham, Maxine. *Spike Milligan: His Part In Our Lives* (London: Robson Books, 2002).

Chapter 9

1 *Cavanagh, John*. "Delia Derbyshire: On Our Wavelength" (*Boazine*, July 1998) http://delia-derbyshire.org/interview_ boa.php.

2 Xenakis, Ian. *Formalized Music, Thought and Mathematics in Composition* (Sheffield, MA: Pendragon Press, 1971).

3 De La Garza, Alejandro. "How Electric Cars Could Craft the Soundscape of the Future" (*Time Magazine*, April 6, 2021). https://time.com/5951773/electric-car-sound-future/.

4 "Orchestra of Silence Part 1: Entering the Future." YouTube. https://www.youtube.com/watch?app=desktop&v=ctUY 7wZayyM.

5   Schafer, R. Murray. *The Soundscape: Our Sonic Environment and the Tuning of the World* (New York: Simon & Schuster, 1993).

6   Schafer, R. Murray. "I Have Never Seen a Sound" Keynote address to the 12th International Congress of Sound and Vibration, 2005. *Environmental & Architectural Phenomenology*, Vol. 17. pg. 10–15.

7   Haynes, Todd. *The Velvet Underground*. Apple TV, 2001.

8   Arnal, Luc H. "Why is the brain disturbed by harsh sounds?" (*Science Daily*, September 20, 2019) https://www.sciencedaily.com/releases/2019/09/190920111349.htm.

Chapter 10

1   McDermott, John and Kramer, Eddie. *Hendrix: Setting the Record Straight* (New York: Grand Central Publishing, 1992).

2   Muggs, Joe. "Radiophonic Workshop: The Shadowy Pioneers of Electronic Sound" (*The Guardian*, November 23, 2013) www.theguardian.com/music/2013/nov/23/radiophonic-workshop-bbc-doctor-who.

3   Radio One. Keeping It Peel, www.bbc.co.uk/radio1/johnpeel/artists/b/broadcast/.

Chapter 11

1   "Soundhouse." May 12, 1993. *Doctor Who Magazine*, 199.

2   Murray, Andy. November 2008. "Delia Derbyshire: the lost tapes," *Wire*, 297, p. 12.

3   BBC. 2010. "Sculptress of Sound: The Lost Works of Delia Derbyshire" https://www.bbc.co.uk/programmes/b00rl2ky.

4   Cavanaugh, John. "Delia Derbyshire: On Our Wavelength"
    (*Boazine* July 2008). Accessed from http://www.delia-derbysh
    ire.org/interview_boa.php.

5   Howell, Peter. *Radiophonic Times* (Edinburgh,
    Scotland: Obverse Books, 2021).

6   The White Files, https://whitefiles.org/rwb/2/index.htm.